BIASES

Biased: 50 Powerful
Cognitive Biases

+

101 Biases in Banking and
Finance

Copyright © Henry Priest

May 2019

CONTENTS

Book 1: Biased

More Intelligent ≠ More Rational	1
Active Choice	6
Anchoring Bias	7
Asymmetric Dominance (Decoy)	8
Automatic Enrolment	9
Availability Bias	10
Channel Factors	11
Choice Overload	12
Choosing Vs. Rejecting	13
Compromise Effect	14
Confirmation Bias	15
Conservatism Bias	16
Construal Levels	17
Decision Points	18
Defaults: Opt-In Vs. Opt-Out	19
Designating Money	20
Endowment Effect	21
Expert Intuition	22
Financial Impatience	23
Framing: Gain Vs. Loss (Loss Aversion)	25
Framing: Narrow Framing	26
Framing: Pay-Per-Day	27
Free – Power of	28
Goal Visibility	29

Grouping	30
Halo Effect	31
Hedonic Editing	33
Herd Behaviour	34
Inside View	35
Mindset: Choice Vs. Evaluation	36
Mindset: Deliberative Vs. Implemental	37
Money Illusion	38
Multi-Stage Decisions	39
Overconfidence	41
Payment Depreciation	42
Perceived Progress	43
Planning Fallacy	44
Pre-Commitment	45
Priming Effect	46
Representativeness Heuristic	47
Salience – Pain Of Payment	48
Salience – Self Identity	49
Social Norms	50
Status Quo Bias	51
Sunk Cost Effect	52
Temptation Bundling	53
Transaction Decoupling	54
Transference of Gain	55
Transference of Loss	56
Underestimating	57
WYSIATI	58
NOTES	60

Book 2: 101 Biases in Banking and Finance

Bias in Banking and Financial Services

1. Action Bias
2. Active Choice
3. Actor–Observer Bias
4. Affect Heuristic
5. Altruism
6. Ambiguity (Uncertainty) Aversion
7. Anchoring (Heuristic)
8. Anchoring Bias
9. Availability Bias
10. Availability Heuristic
11. Bounded Rationality
12. Certainty Effect
13. Certainty/Possibility Effects
14. Channel Factors
15. Choice Overload
16. Choice Overload Or Overchoice
17. Choosing Vs. Rejecting
18. Cognitive Bias
19. Cognitive Dissonance
20. Commitment
21. Compromise Effect

22. Confirmation Bias
23. Confirmation Bias
24. Conjunction Fallacy
25. Conservatism Bias
26. Construal Levels
27. Control Premium
28. Decision Fatigue
29. Decision Points
30. Decision Staging
31. Decoy Effect
32. Default (Option/Setting)
33. Default Bias
34. Diversification Bias
35. Dual-Self Model
36. Ego Depletion
37. Elimination-By-Aspects
38. (Hot-Cold) Empathy Gap
39. Endowment Effect
40. Expert Intuition
41. Fairness
42. Fast And Frugal
43. Financial Impatience
44. Framing Effect
45. Framing: Loss Framing
46. Framing: Pay-Per-Day
47. Free – Power Of Free
48. (Behavioral) Game Theory
49. Goal Visibility
50. Grouping
51. Habit
52. Halo Effect

53. Hedonic Adaptation
54. Hedonic Editing
55. Herd Behaviour
56. Heuristic
57. Honesty
58. Identity Economics
59. Ikea Effect
60. Incentives
61. Inequity Aversion
62. Inertia
63. Information Avoidance
64. Inside View
65. Law Of Small Numbers
66. Loss Aversion
67. Mental Accounting
68. Mental Accounting
69. Mindless Eating
70. Mindset: Choice Vs. Evaluation
71. Mindset: Deliberative Vs. Implemental
72. Money Illusion
73. Multi-Stage Decisions
74. Myopic Loss Aversion
75. Naive Allocation
76. Narrow Framing
77. Optimism Bias
78. Opt-In Vs. Opt-Out
79. Overconfidence
80. Overconfidence (Effect)
81. Pain Of Paying
82. Payment Depreciation
83. Perceived Progress

84. Planning Fallacy
85. Pre-Commitment
86. Preference
87. Preference Reversal
88. Priming (Conceptual)
89. Priming Effect
90. (Myopic) Procrastination
91. Projection Bias
92. Representativeness Heuristic
93. Salience – Self Identity
94. Salience - The Pain Of Payment
95. Scarcity (Psychology Of)
96. Social Norms
97. Status Quo Bias
98. Sunk Cost Fallacy
99. Temptation Bundling
100. Underestimating
101. WYSIATI

Book 1

x

We like to think of ourselves as rational beings. But how rational are we, really?

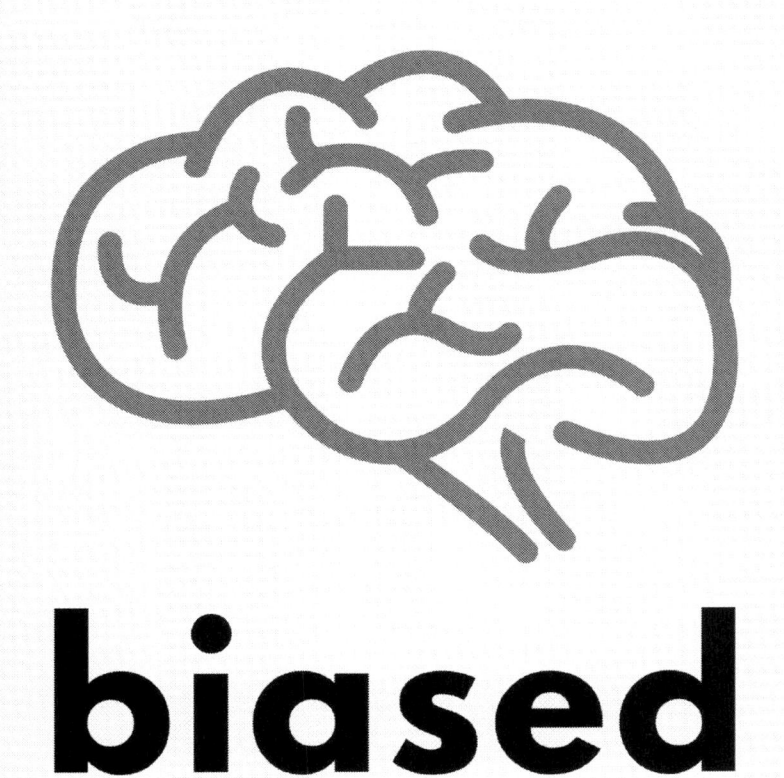

biased

50 Powerful Cognitive Biases That Impair Our Judgment

---

by Henry Priest

Biased

If we want to have meaningful and deeper engagements at our work places and home, we have to understand how people's minds work and how they make their decisions.

Research in psychology and economics has found that human beings are systematically biased. Not only do they misjudge situations, but they do it in fairly regular patterns.

Fortunately, as Nobel laureate Daniel Kahneman says, "we can improve our ability to identify and understand errors of judgment and choice in others, and eventually in ourselves. An accurate diagnosis may suggest an intervention to limit the damage that bad judgments and choices often cause".

This compilation presents behavioral economics research findings on 50 famous cognitive biases that impair our judgment.

Henry Priest
May 2019

BIASED

50 Powerful Cognitive Biases
That Impair Our Judgment

More Intelligent
≠ More Rational

The more intelligent a person is, the more rational she is. That sounds like good common sense. But is that really so? Unfortunately, "smarter" is not always equivalent to "more reasonable". Research suggests that intelligence and rationality are weakly correlated. Or, to put it simply, being more intelligent doesn't necessarily mean you're more rational.

Take the case of Linda. One of the earliest and most influential studies exploring the phenomenon was conducted in the 1970s by psychologists Daniel Kahneman and Amos Tversky. In one of their tests, they had university students read a personality sketch about an individual named Linda:

> *"Linda is 31 years old, single, outspoken and very bright. She majored in philosophy. As a student, she was deeply concerned with issues of discrimination and social justice, and also participated in antinuclear demonstrations."*

The participants were then asked to judge which one of the following two statements was more likely to be true:

> (A) Linda is a bank teller
> (B) Linda is a bank teller and is active in the feminist movement

Eighty-five percent of the volunteers selected (B).

We replicated the study among banking professionals. Surprisingly, 77% of respondents selected (B), and only 23% selected (A).

The problem presented in the above choice is called '*conjunction fallacy*', which is when we mistakenly believe that two events occurring together is more probable than only one of those events occurring. The fact is that there isn't any evidence in the personality sketch that proves that Linda is both a bank teller and a feminist. So statement 'A' should have been the more logical choice.

But four out of five people chose otherwise. This means that even experienced agents like bankers, who are supposed to be trained to be rational thinkers or decision makers, are really not so.

As you could see, Kahneman and Amos Tversky's studies revealed that even intelligent people can have irrational thoughts and beliefs. Our own study corroborated the findings among trained banking professionals. The problem is, instead of using reason or rational thinking, we often resort to intuition when making economic decisions.

Hope for the irrational

Researchers in psychology and economics have found that human beings are systematically irrational. Not only do they misjudge situations, but they do it in fairly predictable patterns.

If you're a banker of average intelligence who also entertains highly irrational thoughts, the bad news is that you can't improve your intelligence. But, the good news is that you can improve rationality through training. It's good to know that even the least rational among us can learn to think more reasonably. We could design training programs to help weed out our irrational biases. Though it is not possible to eliminate all our biases, training can certainly reduce the number of biases that we suffer from and/or reduce their severity/frequency, and thereby make our decisions more reasoned and logical.

Biases to Watch Out For

Conjunction fallacy is just one of the many biases that human beings, including MSME loan officers, suffer from. Researchers collect lists of people's biases, 175 of which are featured on Wikipedia.

If we are aware about cognitive biases, chances are that we will notice them in others and eventually in our own behavior. An accurate diagnosis may suggest an intervention to limit the damage that bad judgments and choices often cause.

In This Volume

This volume is a compilation of select academic research by eminent social psychologists and behavioral economists as easy-to-use tools or 'Biases-in-Action' to help people in general, and loan officers in particular, deal with their bounded rationality and make better decisions.

Cognitive Biases

ACTIVE CHOICE

The Bias in Brief

Highlighting the fact that a decision needs to be made increases the attention paid to the decision-making process. This is especially useful for choices which are typically passive (e.g. getting vaccinated, renewing a gym plan, donating organs). Enhanced active choice refers to the presentation of options that highlight the cost of making a "no" choice.

The Bias in Action

Rather than waiting for individuals to get preventive vaccination, they could be actively asked whether they intend to get vaccinated (active choice). Alternately, they could be presented with two options – (a) Yes, I will get vaccinated and protect me and my family, or (b) No, I am willing to expose me and my family to the risk of the disease.

The rate of getting vaccinated increased with active choice, and further increased with enhanced active choice.

References

Keller, P. A., Harlam, B., Loewenstein, G., & Volpp, K. G. (2011). Enhanced active choice: A new method to motivate behavior change. Journal of Consumer Psychology, 21(4), 376–383.

ANCHORING BIAS

The Bias in Brief

Numerical judgments tend to be influenced by prominent numbers that are available in the context. These prominent numbers – called anchors – need not even be relevant to the judgment.

The Bias in Action

Two groups of people were asked to estimate the population of Perth, Australia. Before estimating, one group was asked whether they thought the population was greater or less than 50,000. The second group was asked whether they thought the population was greater or less than 10,000,000. The actual estimates provided by the second group were significantly higher.

References

Tversky, A., & Kahneman, D. (1974). Judgment under uncertainty: Heuristics and biases. Science, 185(4157), 1124–1131.

ASYMMETRIC DOMINANCE (DECOY)

The Bias in Brief

Consider two options that vary on two attributes. A is better than B on attribute one, but not as good on attribute two. Adding a third option, B*, that is worse than B on both attributes shifts choices towards B. B* can be called a decoy because it is not really preferred but shifts choices among the other two.

The Bias in Action

A consumer is unable to choose between two headphones. Headphone 'A' has a sound quality index of 100 and a comfort rating of 50. Headphone 'B' has a sound quality index of 50 and a comfort rating of 100. The addition of a third (inferior) headphone 'B*' with 40 sound quality index and a 90 comfort rating will increase his likelihood of choosing B.

References

Huber, J., Payne, J. W., & Puto, C. (1982). Adding asymmetrically dominated alternatives: Violations of regularity and the similarity hypothesis. Journal of consumer research, 9(1), 90–98.

AUTOMATIC ENROLMENT

The Bias in Brief

Automatically enrolling people in benefit programs or provident funds but giving them the option of withdrawing increases the likelihood that they will continue to participate.

The Bias in Action

Company A requires all employees who want to participate in their benefits program to sign a form and send it to the human resources department. Company B automatically enrolls all employees into an identical benefits program, but allows them to withdraw with no penalties by signing a form and sending it to the human resources department. In the long run, company B has a significantly higher participation rate in its benefits programs.

References

Madrian, B. C., & Shea, D. F. (2001). The power of suggestion: Inertia in 401 (k) participation and savings behavior. The Quarterly Journal of Economics, 116(4), 1149–1187.

AVAILABILITY BIAS

The Bias in Brief

The availability bias is a mental shortcut that relies on immediate examples that come to mind when evaluating a specific situation.

The Bias in Action

One of the best-known studies of availability suggests that awareness of your own biases can contribute to peace in marriages, and probably in other joint projects. In a famous study, spouses were asked, "How large was your personal contribution to keeping the place tidy, in percentages?" They also answered similar questions about "taking out the garbage," "initiating social engagements," etc.

Would the self-estimated contributions add up to 100%, or more, or less? As expected, the self-assessed contributions added up to more than 100%. The explanation is a simple availability bias: both spouses remember their own individual efforts and contributions much more clearly than those of the other, and the difference in availability leads to a difference in judged frequency.

References

Kahneman, Daniel, 2013, Thinking Fast and Slow, Publisher: Farrar, Straus and Giroux; Reprint edition (2 April 2013), ISBN-10: 0374533555, ISBN-13: 978-0374533557

CHANNEL FACTORS

The Bias in Brief

Features of the physical space and surroundings in a task oriented environment can either facilitate or hinder the achievement of the task. Eliminating features that hinder the task will increase the likelihood of completion.

The Bias in Action

Two groups of low-income consumers heard a (identical) seminar about the importance of opening bank accounts. At the end of the seminar, one group was given the forms needed to open bank accounts, while the second was given forms as well as a map and directions to the bank. Significantly more people from the second group opened bank accounts.

References

Mullainathan, S., & Shafir, E. (2009). Savings policy and decision-making in low-income households. In M. Barr & R. Blank (Eds.), Insufficient funds: Savings, assets, credit, and banking among low-income households. Russell Sage Foundation Press (pp. 121–145).

CHOICE OVERLOAD

The Bias in Brief

"Choice Overload", is a term describing a cognitive process in which people have a difficult time making a decision when faced with many options. The term was first introduced by Alvin Toffler in his 1970 book, Future Shock.

The Bias in Action

In 2000, psychologists Sheena Iyengar and Mark Lepper published a remarkable study. On one day, shoppers at an upscale food market saw a display table with 24 varieties of gourmet jam. Those who sampled the spreads received a coupon for $1 off any jam. On another day, shoppers saw a similar table, except that only six varieties of the jam were on display. The large display attracted more interest than the small one. But when the time came to purchase, people who saw the large display were one-tenth as likely to buy as people who saw the small display.

References

Barry Schwartz, The Paradox of Choice: Why More Is Less (Harper Perennial, 2005),

CHOOSING VS. REJECTING

The Bias in Brief

The manner in which people are asked to choose between two options can change the information they use in making the decision. In particular, asking people to choose between A and B results on their focusing on reasons to choose (positive aspects), while asking them to reject A or B results on their focusing on reasons to reject (negative aspects).

The Bias in Action

A manager is looking for hiring one of two job candidates. Mr. A is average on all four relevant attributes, while Ms. B is outstanding on two and weak on the other two. When the manager chooses between the two, B tends to be preferred over A (there are more reasons to choose B). When the manager is rejecting one of the two, B tends to get rejected more often (there are more reasons to reject B).

References

Shafir, E. (1993). Choosing versus rejecting: Why some options are both better and worse than others. Memory & Cognition, 21(4), 546–556.

COMPROMISE EFFECT

The Bias in Brief

When people choose between three options that vary along two dimensions, the option in the middle (which is average on both dimensions) tends to get chosen more often. Conversely, the likelihood of choice of an option can be increased by making it the "compromise" option. This effect is particularly strong for options where it is difficult to evaluate quality.

The Bias in Action

A gas station sold two types of petrol - 89 and 91 octane grade petrol. The sales of 91 went up after they now introduced a 94 octane grade, because 91 now became the "compromise" option.

In most coffee/soft-drink/pop-corn shops where the refreshment is offered in three sizes, the medium is the most popular size.

References

Simonson, I. (1989). Choice Based on Reasons: The Case of Attraction and Compromise Effects. Journal of Consumer Research, 16(2), 158–174.

CONFIRMATION BIAS

The Bias in Brief

The tendency to interpret new evidence as confirmation of one's existing beliefs or theories.

The Bias in Action

When asked, "Is Sam friendly?" different instances of Sam's behavior will come to mind than would if you had been asked "Is Sam unfriendly?" Contrary to the rules of philosophers of science, who advise testing hypotheses by trying to refute them, people (and scientists, quite often) seek data that are likely to be compatible with the beliefs they currently hold. The confirmatory bias favors uncritical acceptance of suggestions and exaggeration of the likelihood of extreme and improbable events.

References

Kahneman, Daniel, 2013, Thinking Fast and Slow, Publisher: Farrar, Straus and Giroux; Reprint edition (2 April 2013), ISBN-10: 0374533555, ISBN-13: 978-0374533557

CONSERVATISM BIAS

The Bias in Brief

Conservatism describes human belief revision in which persons over-weigh the prior distribution (base rate) and under-weigh new sample evidence when compared to Bayesian belief-revision.

The Bias in Action

In finance, evidence has been found that investors under-react to corporate events, consistent with conservatism. This includes announcements of earnings, changes in dividends, and stock splits.

References

Edwards, Ward. "Conservatism in Human Information Processing (excerpted)". In Daniel Kahneman, Paul Slovic and Amos Tversky. (1982). Judgment under uncertainty: Heuristics and biases. New York: Cambridge University Press. ISBN 978-0521284141 Original work published 1968.

CONSTRUAL LEVELS

The Bias in Brief

When events are to happen in the future, people view them in terms of their higher level benefits. When the same event is to happen now, it is viewed in terms of concrete details. For events that have high levels of abstract benefits but involve a lot of concrete detail (effort), this results in a diminished attractiveness of the event as it comes closer in time.

The Bias in Action

Neel was intrigued by the possibility of learning a new language and enrolled for Japanese classes that would happen in two months. After two months passed, the inconvenience of taking public transit, purchasing books, and giving up on leisure activities seemed too much, and he decided to cancel his registration.

References

Trope, Y., & Liberman, N. (2003). Temporal construal. Psychological Review, 110(3), 403–421.

DECISION POINTS

The Bias in Brief

People often start consumption episodes with a decision to consume, but then passively continue consumption till they hit a constraint. Inserting an opportunity to pause and think about the consumption in an active manner (a decision point) will increase vigilance and hence, the likelihood that consumption stops. Decision points could take the form of reminders, small transaction costs, or physical partitions.

The Bias in Action

Mr. X is given a large bucket of popcorn. Mr. Y has the same quantity of popcorn in four equal bags. Assuming that they are both conscious of the need to control consumption, Mr. Y will consume less than Mr. X.

References

Soman, D., Xu, J., & Cheema, A. (2010). A theory of decision points. Rotman Magazine, Winter, 64–68.

DEFAULTS: OPT-IN VS. OPT-OUT

The Bias in Brief

The default choice in any decision task refers to the outcome that would happen if the individual did not make a choice. If a situation where people choosing not to choose is high (low opt-in), making a desired outcome the default (with an opt-out) will increase the likelihood of it being chosen.

The Bias in Action

In Canada, citizens wishing to donate organs must follow a procedure to get registered. Is France, the assumption is that everybody will donate organs, but citizens wishing to not donate can follow a procedure to get de-registered. Organ donation rates are significantly higher in France than in Canada.

In country A, credit card applicants must sign a consent allowing for their mailing address to be shared on a mailing list. In country B, applicants need to sign to prevent their addresses from being on a mailing list. The average citizen in country A receives a lot less junk mail than in country B.

References

Johnson, E. J., & Goldstein, D. (2003). Do Defaults Save Lives? Science, 302 (5649), 1338–1339.

DESIGNATING MONEY

The Bias in Brief

Money that is designated toward a particular cause is more likely to be spent on that cause. Designating can be achieved by physically segregating money into separate envelopes.

The Bias in Action

Daily wage earners in India were given a savings target Rs. 40 per day. Some of them were encouraged to earmark the Rs. 40 by putting it in a separate envelope. These wage earners were more likely to save.

References

Soman, D., & Cheema, A. (2011). Earmarking and Partitioning: Increasing Saving by Low-Income Households. Journal of Marketing Research, 48(Special), S14–22.

ENDOWMENT EFFECT

The Bias in Brief

Endowment effect (also known as divestiture aversion and related to the mere ownership effect in social psychology) is the hypothesis that people ascribe more value to things merely because they own them.

The Bias in Action

Suppose you hold a ticket to a sold-out concert by a popular band, which you bought at the regular price of $200. You are an avid fan and would have been willing to pay up to $500 for the ticket. Now you have your ticket and you learn on the Internet that richer or more desperate fans are offering $3,000. Would you sell? If you resemble most of the audience at sold-out events you do not sell. Your lowest selling price is above $3,000 and your maximum buying price is $500. This is an example of an endowment effect

References

Kahneman, Daniel, 2013, Thinking Fast and Slow, Publisher: Farrar, Straus and Giroux; Reprint edition (2 April 2013), ISBN-10: 0374533555, ISBN-13: 978-0374533557

EXPERT INTUITION

The Bias in Brief

Valid intuitions develop when experts have learned to recognize familiar elements in a new situation and to act in a manner that is appropriate to it. Herbert Simon says "The situation has provided a cue; this cue has given the expert access to information stored in memory, and the information provides the answer. Intuition is nothing more and nothing less than recognition."

The Bias in Action

The physician who makes a complex diagnosis after a single glance at a patient. Expert intuition strikes us as magical, but it is not. Indeed, each of us performs feats of intuitive expertise many times each day. Most of us are pitch-perfect in detecting anger in the first word of a telephone call, recognize as we enter a room that we were the subject of the conversation, and quickly react to subtle signs that the driver of the car in the next lane is dangerous. Our everyday intuitive abilities are no less marvelous than the striking insights of an experienced firefighter or physician—only more common.

References

Kahneman, Daniel, 2013, Thinking Fast and Slow, Publisher: Farrar, Straus and Giroux; Reprint edition (2

April 2013), ISBN-10: 0374533555, ISBN-13: 978-0374533557

FINANCIAL IMPATIENCE

The Bias in Brief

Prevalence of fast-food restaurants in the social ecology are associated with greater financial impatience at the national, neighborhood, and individual level.

The Bias in Action

Study 1 shows that the proliferation of fast-food restaurants over the past 3 decades in the developed world was associated with a historic shift in financial impatience, as manifested in precipitously declining household savings rates. Study 2 finds that households saved less when living in neighborhoods with a higher concentration of fast-food restaurants relative to full-service restaurants.

With a direct measure of individuals' delay discounting preferences, Study 3 confirms that a higher concentration of fast-food restaurants within one's neighborhood is associated with greater financial impatience. In line with a causal relationship, Study 4 reveals that recalling a recent fast-food, as opposed to full-service, dining experience at restaurants within the same neighborhood induced greater delay discounting, which was mediated behaviorally by how quickly participants completed the recall task itself.

Finally, Study 5 demonstrates that pedestrians walking down the same urban street exhibited greater delay discounting in their choice of financial reward if they were surveyed in front of a fast-food restaurant, compared to a full-service restaurant.

Collectively, these data indicate a link between the prevalence of fast food and financial impatience across multiple levels of analysis, and suggest the plausibility of fast food having a reinforcing effect on financial impatience. The present investigation highlights how the pervasiveness of organizational cues in the everyday social ecology can have a far-ranging influence.

References

Fast Food and Financial Impatience: A Socio-ecological Approach Sanford E. DeVoe, Julian House, and Chen-Bo Zhong University of Toronto, Journal of Personality and Social Psychology, 2013, Vol. 105, No. 3, 476–494

FRAMING: GAIN VS. LOSS (LOSS AVERSION)

The Bias in Brief

Presenting the same outcome as a loss has a greater psychological effect than presenting it as a gain.

The Bias in Action

A 3% credit card surcharge was framed as a cash discount – people who pay by credit card paid the full bill amount (which included the 3%), while people who paid in cash got a 3% discount. Now the price difference between paying by credit cards and cash was seen as more acceptable.

In one neighborhood, employees of a utility company tried to convince households to purchase energy-efficient appliances by saying "If you use these appliances, you will save $10 per month." In a second neighborhood, this statement was changed to "If you fail to use these appliances, you will lose $10 per month." The likelihood of purchasing energy-efficient appliances was significantly greater in the second neighborhood.

References

Kahneman, D., & Tversky, A. (1979). Prospect Theory: An Analysis of Decision under Risk. Econometrica, 47(2), 263–291.

FRAMING: NARROW FRAMING

The Bias in Brief

Narrow framing, by contrast, is the phenomenon documented in experimental settings whereby, when people are offered a new gamble, they evaluate it in isolation, separately from their other risks. In other words, they act as if they get utility directly from the outcome of the gamble, even if the gamble is just one of many that determine their overall wealth risk. This contrasts with traditional specifications, in which the agent would only get utility from the outcome of the gamble indirectly, via its contribution to his total wealth.

The Bias in Action

We may be able to improve our understanding of how people evaluate stock market risk by looking at how they evaluate risk in experimental settings. More specifically, this approach argues that loss aversion and narrow framing, two of the most important ideas to emerge from the experimental literature on decision-making under risk, may also play an important role in the stock market setting.

References

The Loss Aversion / Narrow Framing Approach to the Equity Premium Puzzle, Nicholas Barberis and Ming

Huang Yale University and Cornell University, October 2005

FRAMING: PAY-PER-DAY

The Bias in Brief

Presenting a large dollar amount as an equivalent number of dollars per day could increase the acceptability of this expense. However, this effect reverses if the per day expense is very large.

The Bias in Action

A charity asked individuals to donate $350 towards a certain cause. Subsequently, they changed their request and framed the money as "less than a dollar a day". Donations increased significantly.

References

Gourville, J. T. (1998). Pennies-a-day: The effect of temporal reframing on transaction evaluation. Journal of Consumer Research, 24(4), 395–403.

FREE – POWER OF

The Bias in Brief

The word "free" captures our attention in a powerful way. Free is in a league of its own.

The Bias in Action

Behavioral economist Dan Ariely wrote about a study in his book Predictably Irrational in which they gave people the option to choose between two offers. One was a $10 Amazon gift certificate for free; the other was a $20 gift card available for $7. More people chose the $10 gift card even though the other option provided more value.

References

Predictably Irrational, Dan Ariely, Harper Perennial; 2010

GOAL VISIBILITY

The Bias in Brief

When people are in the middle of a goal-oriented task, they work harder towards accomplishing the goal when it is in sight. Consequently, reminding people of their goal or making the goal more salient or visual increases motivation.

The Bias in Action

Competitive swimmers swim faster on laps in which they face the end point of the race, and slower when they are swimming away from the endpoint.

Putting photographs of children on savings envelopes increased the saving rate of parents who were saving for their children's education.

References

Cheema, A., & Bagchi, R. (2011). The Effect of Goal Visualization on Goal Pursuit: Implications for Individuals and Managers. Journal of Marketing, 75(2), 109–123.

GROUPING

The Bias in Brief

Grouping multiple objects into separate categories increases the nature of the choice process between those alternatives.

The Bias in Action

A mutual fund company sorted their offering of mutual funds along the country of origin. As a result, their customers diversified by trying to purchase funds from different countries. When the same set of mutual funds was grouped by the industry type, diversification by country decreased, while diversification by industry increased.

References

Fox, C. R., Ratner, R. K., & Lieb, D. S. (2005). How subjective grouping of options influences choice and allocation: diversification bias and the phenomenon of partition dependence. Journal of Experimental Psychology: General, 134(4), 538–551.

HALO EFFECT

The Bias in Brief

The halo effect is a cognitive bias in which an observer's overall impression of a person, company, brand, or product influences the observer's feelings and thoughts about that entity's character or properties. The halo effect is a specific type of confirmation bias, wherein positive feelings in one area cause ambiguous or neutral traits to be viewed positively. Edward Thorndike originally coined the term referring only to people; however, its use has been greatly expanded especially in the area of brand marketing.

The Bias in Action

A study by Landy & Sigall (1974) demonstrated the halo effect on judgments of intelligence and competence on academic tasks. Sixty male undergraduate students rated the quality of essays which included both well and poorly written samples. One third were presented with a photo of an attractive female as author, another third with that of an unattractive female as author, and the last third were shown neither.

Participants gave significantly better writing evaluations for the more attractive author. On a scale of 1 to 9, the well-written essay by the attractive author received an average of 6.7 while the unattractive author received a

5.9 (with a 6.6 as a control). The gap was larger on the poor essay: the attractive author received an average of 5.2, the control a 4.7, and the unattractive a 2.7, suggesting readers are generally more willing to give physically attractive people the benefit of the doubt when performance is below standard than others.

References

Landy, D; Sigall, H (1974), "Task Evaluation as a Function of the Performers' Physical Attractiveness", Journal of Personality and Social Psychology 29 (3): 299–304, doi:10.1037/h0036018

HEDONIC EDITING

The Bias in Brief

People either integrate or segregate monetary outcomes in order to maximise their psychological impact. In particular:

A single loss is preferred to multiple losses

Multiple gains are preferred to a single gain

In situations where there is a large loss and a small gain, the gain should be separated from the loss (the silver lining principle)

The Bias in Action

A tire shop that charged $200 for tire replacement offered a $10 discount. This small benefit was lost in the context of the large price tag. A second tire shop instead mailed their patrons a $10 gift certificate two weeks after getting their tires replaced. By separating this small gain, they made its psychological value much higher.

References

Thaler, R. H. (1999). Mental accounting matters. Journal of Behavioral Decision Making, 12(3), 183–206.

HERD BEHAVIOUR

The Bias in Brief

The tendency for individuals to mimic the actions (rational or irrational) of a larger group.

The Bias in Action

Herd behavior, as the bubbles illustrate, is usually not a very profitable investment strategy. Investors that employ a herd-mentality investment strategy constantly buy and sell their investment assets in pursuit of the newest and hottest investment trends. For example, if a herd investor hears that internet stocks are the best investments right now, he will free up his investment capital and then dump it on internet stocks. If biotech stocks are all the rage six months later, he'll probably move his money again, perhaps before he has even experienced significant appreciation in his internet investments.

References

INSIDE VIEW

The Bias in Brief

People who have information about an individual case rarely feel the need to know the statistics of the class to which the case belongs.

The Bias in Action

A distinguished lawyer was once asked a question about a reference class: "What is the probability of the defendant winning in cases like this one?" His sharp answer that "every case is unique" was accompanied by a look that made it clear he found my question inappropriate and superficial. A proud emphasis on the uniqueness of cases is also common in medicine, in spite of recent advances in evidence-based medicine that point the other way. Medical statistics and baseline predictions come up with increasing frequency in conversations between patients and physicians.

References

Kahneman, D., & Tversky, A. (1979). Prospect Theory: An Analysis of Decision under Risk. Econometrica, 47(2), 263–291.

MINDSET: CHOICE VS. EVALUATION

The Bias in Brief

A mindset refers to the style with which the human brain processes information. When a person has made a large number of choices, they are more likely to view incoming (unrelated) information as a choice problem.

The Bias in Action

One group of people was asked "which of the following is more prototypical of birds?" by making choices between a large numbers of pairs of birds (e.g. "crow or penguin?"). A second group was asked to evaluate (not choose) the prototypicality of a large number of birds on a scale.

Both groups were shown purchase opportunities where they could choose Product 'A' or Product 'B', or to not choose at all. People who had chosen amongst birds were more likely to choose, and hence make a purchase, than people who merely evaluated.

References

Xu, A. J., & Wyer, R. S. (2008). The Comparative Mind-Set From Animal Comparisons to Increased

Purchase Intentions. Psychological Science, 19(9), 859–864.

MINDSET: DELIBERATIVE VS. IMPLEMENTAL

The Bias in Brief

A mindset refers to the style with which the human brain processes information. When a person has approached a large number of events with a view to getting them done (rather than merely thinking about them), they are more likely to get the next event done.

The Bias in Action

Ms. A and Ms. B both faced a job that was due in three weeks and were asked when they planned to start working on it. Prior to this, Ms. A was asked about the importance of five earlier jobs she had done, while Ms. B was asked how she accomplished five of her recent jobs.

Ms. B was more likely so start working on the new job sooner.

References

Gollwitzer, P. M. (1999). Implementation intentions: strong effects of simple plans. American Psychologist, 54(7), 493–503.

MONEY ILLUSION

The Bias in Brief

Belief that money has a fixed value in terms of its purchasing power, so that, for example, changes in prices represent real gains and losses.

The Bias in Action

Eldar Shafir, Peter A. Diamond, and Amos Tversky (1997) have provided empirical evidence for the existence of the effect and it has been shown to affect behaviour in a variety of experimental and real-world situations.

Shafir et al. also state that money illusion influences economic behaviour in three main ways:

Price stickiness. Money illusion has been proposed as one reason why nominal prices are slow to change even where inflation has caused real prices or costs to rise.

Contracts and laws are not indexed to inflation as frequently as one would rationally expect.

Social discourse, in formal media and more generally, reflects some confusion about real and nominal value.

References

Shafir, E.; Diamond, P. A.; Tversky, A. (1997), "On Money Illusion", Quarterly Journal of Economics 112 (2): 341–374,doi:10.1162/003355397555208

MULTI-STAGE DECISIONS

The Bias in Brief

Presenting the same choice as a multiple stage decision rather than a single stage decision can change the outcome of the choice task.

The Bias in Action

One group of people (A) were told they would play in a lottery which offered a 25% chance of going to the second round. At this round, they were asked to choose between:

Option 1A: Get $300 for sure; Option 2A: 80% chance of winning $450, else nothing

A second group (B) was offered a choice between two gambles:

Option 1B: 25% chance of winning $300, else nothing; Option 2B: 20% chance of winning $450, else nothing

Option 1A is identical to 1B, and 2A is identical to 2B. Yet people in group A prefer 1A over 2A (there is an illusion of certainty) while people in group B prefer 2B to

1A (now $450 appears larger than $300, while the difference between 20% and 25% doesn't seem as large). Hence, presenting a gamble as a two stage decision could create an illusion of certainty and change choice.

A group of friends are deciding which restaurant to go to for dinner. In one version, they are asked to choose between Chinese, Italian, or Thai cuisines. In a second version, they are first asked if they would like Chinese, and if not, whether they would like Thai or Italian. The likelihood of choosing Chinese is significantly greater in the second version.

References

Kahneman, D., & Tversky, A. (1979). Prospect Theory: An Analysis of Decision under Risk. Econometrica, 47(2), 263–291.

OVERCONFIDENCE

The Bias in Brief

A person's subjective confidence in his or her judgments is reliably greater than the objective accuracy of those judgments, especially when confidence is relatively high.

The Bias in Action

Neither the quantity nor the quality of the evidence counts for much in subjective confidence. The confidence that individuals have in their beliefs depends mostly on the quality of the story they can tell about what they see, even if they see little.

We often fail to allow for the possibility that evidence that should be critical to our judgment is missing—what we see is all there is. Furthermore, our associative system tends to settle on a coherent pattern of activation and suppresses doubt and ambiguity.

References

PAYMENT DEPRECIATION

The Bias in Brief

The pain of payment decreases as time passes from the payment. As a result, the strength of the sunk cost effect (a pressure to consume events that have been prepaid for) decreases with time.

The Bias in Action

The attendance rates at a physical fitness centre gradually decline from the time of making an annual membership payment. On the other hand, patrons who make monthly payments show a more stable attendance rate as a function of time.

References

Gourville, J. T., & Soman, D. (1998). Payment depreciation: The behavioral effects of temporally separating payments from consumption. Journal of Consumer Research, 25(2), 160–174.

PERCEIVED PROGRESS

The Bias in Brief

People in a goal-oriented task are more motivated to accomplish the task when they receive feedback about the progress they have made. Their motivation is driven not only by actual levels of progress, but also by their perception of progress.

The Bias in Action

People waiting in a long queue were more likely to continue waiting when the queue took the form of a line that moved as some people were being served, rather than that of a take-a-number-and-wait queue.

Two groups of people were given 400 lines of text to proofread. The first group received 20 pages of 20 lines each; the second group received 40 pages of 10 lines each. Members of the second group found themselves working faster, had a greater perception of progress, and hence were more likely to finish the task.

References

Zhou, R., & Soman, D. (2003). Looking back: Exploring the psychology of queuing and the effect of the number of people behind. Journal of Consumer Research, 29(4), 517–530.

PLANNING FALLACY

The Bias in Brief

Overly optimistic forecasts of the outcome of projects are found everywhere. Planning fallacy refers to plans and forecasts that are unrealistically close to best-case scenarios, which could be improved by consulting the statistics of similar cases

The Bias in Action

A 2005 study examined rail projects undertaken worldwide between 1969 and 1998. In more than 90% of the cases, the number of passengers projected to use the system was overestimated. Even though these passenger shortfalls were widely publicized, forecasts did not improve over those thirty years; on average, planners overestimated how many people would use the new rail projects by 106%, and the average cost overrun was 45%. As more evidence accumulated, the experts did not become more reliant on it.

References

Kahneman, Daniel, 2013, Thinking Fast and Slow, Publisher: Farrar, Straus and Giroux; Reprint edition (2 April 2013), ISBN-10: 0374533555, ISBN-13: 978-0374533557

PRE-COMMITMENT

The Bias in Brief
When people view events that are in the future, they are more likely to be rational and wise about their choices. When the same events are in the present, people act impulsively and make foolish choices. Therefore, the best way of nudging people to make wise choices is to ask them to commit to making those choices for the future.

The Bias in Action
Employees in an organization were asked if they would like to increase their savings rate in the future. Most agreed, and committed to setting aside a proportion of their future salary increase into a separate savings account. These people who were asked to save-more-in-future saved significantly more than people who worked with a traditional financial advisor.

References

Thaler, R. H., & Benartzi, S. (2004). Save More Tomorrow: Using Behavioral Economics to Increase Employee Saving. Journal of Political Economy, 112(1), S164–S187.

PRIMING EFFECT

The Bias in Brief

Our thoughts and our behavior are influenced, much more than we know or want, by the environment of the moment.

The Bias in Action

Consider these two questions: Was Gandhi more or less than 144 years old when he died? How old was Gandhi when he died? Did you produce your estimate by adjusting down from 144? Probably not, but the absurdly high number still affected your estimate. My hunch was that anchoring is a case of suggestion. This is the word we use when someone causes us to see, hear, or feel something by merely bringing it to mind. For example, the question "Do you now feel a slight numbness in your left leg?" always prompts quite a few people to report that their left leg does indeed feel a little strange.

References

Kahneman, Daniel, 2013, Thinking Fast and Slow, Publisher: Farrar, Straus and Giroux; Reprint edition (2 April 2013), ISBN-10: 0374533555, ISBN-13: 978-0374533557

REPRESENTATIVENESS HEURISTIC

The Bias in Brief

The representativeness heuristic is involved when someone says "She will win the election; you can see she is a winner" or "He won't go far as an academic; too many tattoos." We rely on representativeness when we judge the potential leadership of a candidate for office by the shape of his chin or the forcefulness of his speeches.

The Bias in Action

Michael Lewis's bestselling 'Moneyball' is a story about the inefficiency of this mode of prediction. Professional baseball scouts traditionally forecast the success of possible players in part by their build and look. The hero of Lewis's book is Billy Beane, the manager of the Oakland A's, who made the unpopular decision to overrule his scouts and to select players by the statistics of past performance. The players the A's picked were inexpensive, because other teams had rejected them for not looking the part. The team soon achieved excellent results at low cost.

References

Kahneman, Daniel, 2013, Thinking Fast and Slow, Publisher: Farrar, Straus and Giroux; Reprint edition (2

April 2013), ISBN-10: 0374533555, ISBN-13: 978-0374533557

SALIENCE – PAIN OF PAYMENT PROCESS

The Bias in Brief

In addition to the negativity of paying a certain amount, the manner in which the payment is made can create further negativity. Certain methods of payment that are extremely salient (e.g. cash or cheque) feel more painful than others that are not as salient (e.g. auto-pay or direct debit). The pain of payment determines the willingness to spend.

The Bias in Action

When a Laundromat changed from accepting cash to accepting prepaid cards, the number of people running multiple loads of laundry increased.

When a cafeteria in Hong Kong moved from accepting cash to accepting the Octopus (a prepaid electronic card) the sales of desserts and beverages increased.

References

Soman, D. (2001). Effects of payment mechanism on spending behavior: The role of rehearsal and immediacy of payments. Journal of Consumer Research, 27(4), 460–474.

SALIENCE – SELF IDENTITY

The Bias in Brief

Any intervention that increases one's identity as a virtuous person increases the likelihood that they will make virtuous choices. However, it is important that the intervention happens before the choices have to be made.

The Bias in Action

People often misreport (cheat) in domains ranging from tax forms to insurance claims. In most of these situations, people have to sign and declare that the contents of the form are true – but the declaration is made at the end of the form, after all the reporting has been done. When the declaration is made prior to the reporting, the extent of misreporting and cheating significantly declines.

References

Shu, L. L., Mazar, N., Gino, F., Ariely, D., & Bazerman, M. H. (2012). Signing at the beginning makes ethics salient and decreases dishonest self-reports in comparison to signing at the end. Proceedings of the National Academy of Sciences, 109(38), 15197–15200.

SOCIAL NORMS

The Bias in Brief

Making a commitment in the presence of peers increases the likelihood that the commitment will be followed by appropriate action. Also, the presence of peers who have high levels of accomplishment increase the motivation to similarly increase accomplishment.

The Bias in Action

Members of a self help group savings program increase their savings rate when their peers routinely met to discuss progress and outcomes.

Households in the UK were sent letters encouraging them to pay taxes on time. When these letters included a statement of peer performance (e.g. "9/10 people in the UK pay their taxes on time") the letters were more effective.

References

Kast, F., Meier, S., and Pomeranz, D. (2012). Under-savers anonymous: Evidence on self-help groups and peer pressure as a savings commitment device, Discussion Paper series, Forschungsinstitut zur Zukunft der Arbeit, No. 6311, http://nbnresolving.de/urn:nbn:de:101:1-201204239864

STATUS QUO BIAS

The Bias in Brief

The asymmetric intensity of the motives to avoid losses and to achieve gains is an ever present feature of negotiations, especially of renegotiations of an existing contract, the typical situation in labor negotiations and in international discussions of trade or arms limitations.

The existing terms define reference points, and a proposed change in any aspect of the agreement is inevitably viewed as a concession that one side makes to the other. Loss aversion creates an asymmetry that makes agreements difficult to reach.

The Bias in Action

Reforms commonly include grandfather clauses that protect current stake-holders—for example, when the existing workforce is reduced by attrition rather than by dismissals, or when cuts in salaries and benefits apply only to future workers. Loss aversion is a powerful conservative force that favors minimal changes from the status quo in the lives of both institutions and individuals. This conservatism helps keep us stable in our neighborhood, our marriage, and our job; it is the gravitational force that holds our life together near the reference point.

References

Kahneman, Daniel, 2013, Thinking Fast and Slow, Publisher: Farrar, Straus and Giroux; 2013.

SUNK COST EFFECT

The Bias in Brief

People who have prepaid for a consumption opportunity are driven to consume so that they can satisfactorily close their mental account without a loss. The drive to consume will be greater when the amount prepaid is higher.

The Bias in Action

Jack and Jill both had rink side seats for a basketball game. On the day of the game, there was a heavy snowstorm and the game was being shown on TV. Jill decided to stay home, while Jack braved the treacherous conditions to attend the game. Jill had received her ticket as a gift, while Jack had paid $100 for it.

References

Thaler, R. H. (1999). Mental accounting matters. Journal of Behavioral Decision Making, 12(3), 183–206.

TEMPTATION BUNDLING

The Bias in Brief

Creating a mechanism where people can only consume an indulgence while they consume a virtuous product will increase the likelihood that the virtuous product is consumed.

The Bias in Action

Two groups of people were encouraged to exercise more often. One of the groups was allowed to watch their favorite TV show only in the gym room, while the other had no such constraint. People in the first group exercised more because they could bundle their temptation along with the exercise.

References

Milkman, K., Minson, J., & Volpp, K. (2013). Holding the Hunger Games Hostage at the Gym: An Evaluation of Temptation Bundling. The Wharton School Research Paper No. 45. Available at SSRN: http://ssrn.com/abstract=2183859

TRANSACTION DECOUPLING

The Bias in Brief

The strength of the sunk cost effect can be weakened if the physical form of a transaction makes it difficult to associate a price tag with every unit of consumption.

The Bias in Action

Jack and Jill both had season tickets for their favorite basketball team. While they paid the same amount, the physical formats of the season tickets were different. Jack's tickets took the form of a booklet of coupons – one coupon for each game. Jill's ticket took the form of a membership card which she showed every time she entered the stadium.

On the day of one of the games, there was a heavy snowstorm and the game was being shown on TV. Jill decided to stay home, while Jack braved the treacherous conditions to attend the game. The physical format of his ticket made it easier to realize that he would be "wasting" money by not attending.

References

Soman, D., & Gourville, J. T. (2001). Transaction decoupling: How Price bundling affects the decision to consume. Journal of Marketing Research, 38(1), 30–44

TRANSFERENCE OF GAIN

The Bias in Brief

Where gains arising out of agents' actions can be transferred to their principal or to a third party, (e.g. the joint stock company, the government, the public sector company or a middleman), personal losses to agents always seem larger than the potential gains to their principals.

The Bias in Action

This can make agents extremely risk-averse or indifferent and depress initiative.

References

TRANSFERENCE OF LOSS

The Bias in Brief

Where losses arising out of agents' actions can be transferred to their principal, or to a third party, (e.g. the joint stock company, the government, the public sector company or even a scapegoat), personal gains to agents loom larger than the potential losses to their principals.

The Bias in Action

This can flip agents to be risk-seeking even in the gain domain.

References

UNDERESTIMATING

The Bias in Brief

Paradoxically, it is easier to construct a coherent story when you know little. Our comforting conviction that the world makes sense rests on a secure foundation: our almost unlimited ability to ignore our ignorance.

The Bias in Action

Consider the story of Google. Two creative graduate students in the computer science department at Stanford University come up with a superior way of searching information on the Internet. They seek and obtain funding to start a company and make a series of decisions that work out well. Within a few years, the company they started is one of the most valuable stocks in America, and the two former graduate students are among the richest people on the planet.

On one memorable occasion, they were lucky, which makes the story even more compelling: a year after founding Google, they were willing to sell their company for less than $1 million, but the buyer said the price was too high. Mentioning the single lucky incident actually makes it easier to underestimate the multitude of ways in which luck affected the outcome.

References

Kahneman, Daniel, 2013, Thinking Fast and Slow, Publisher: Farrar, Straus and Giroux; 2013

WYSIATI

The Bias in Brief

Jumping to conclusions on the basis of limited evidence is very important to an understanding of intuitive thinking. The cumbersome abbreviation WYSIATI stands for "what you see is all there is".

The Bias in Action

When information is scarce, which is a common occurrence, our mind operates as a machine for jumping to conclusions.

Consider the following: "Will Linda be a good leader? She is intelligent and strong…" An answer quickly came to your mind, and it was yes. You picked the best answer based on the very limited information available, but you jumped the gun. What if the next two adjectives were "corrupt" and "cruel"?

References

Kahneman, Daniel, 2013, Thinking Fast and Slow, Publisher: Farrar, Straus and Giroux; Reprint edition (2 April 2013), ISBN-10: 0374533555, ISBN-13: 978-0374533557

NOTES

Book 2

101 BIASES IN BANKING & FINANCE

How Cognitive Biases Impair
Professional Decisions

BY HENRY PRIEST

101 Biases in Banking & Finance

How Powerful Cognitive Biases Impair Professional Decisions

Bias in Banking and Finance

Behavioral economists have shown that financial decisions are likely to be subject to decision making bias. Given the nature of modern banking, which is getting increasingly complex with more and more exotic financial products and complex bundling and securitization, rational decision making is becoming increasingly difficult. This is because lay customers default to System-1 decision making and use compensating strategies in the face of complexity such as rule of thumb and heuristics. Incentives by financial institutions were aggressively designed to ramp up assets to cope with the torrent of capital flow prior to the financial crisis may have created a choice architecture which diverged from rational decision making.

The sub-prime housing market and related mortgage products was guided by a rule of thumb which for decision making - *'invest in property'*. This philosophy is likely to have guided first-time buyers to make quick, ill-thought through, decisions as properties were seen as 'flying off the shelf'.

Many of these mortgage applicants neither read nor understood the terms of their contract. In the drive for sales, sellers of mortgages also used unreliable rule of thumb guidelines to make quick judgments about creditworthiness. Thus, both parties in the increasingly 'toxic' sub-prime market made less than rational decisions.

Evidently it was not in their self-interest. But did they really know? One can argue that transactions were based on a false reality with little understating of how the market moves.

Buyers and sellers of financial products must rely much more on trust. That is how the market is designed and is working. But when economic 'bubbles' start forming and a financial market 'gathers steam' the pressure is on to buy or sell, and the probability of a rational choice declines.

This raises the question of how we can educate bankers and brokers and their customers on what impairs their rational thinking and how they can step away from the landmines in decision making.

This compilation features 101 cognitive biases and heuristics that are generally found in the banking and financial services sector. Knowing these biases will help readers understand how they work, identify biases in others and then finally recognize them in their own working. Once we identify a bias influencing our thought, it becomes easy to plan and execute a remedy to neutralize its ill effects and uphold rationality.

101 Biases in Banking & Finance

ACTION BIAS

The Bias in Brief

People have an impulse to act in order to gain a sense of control over a situation and eliminate a problem.

This has been termed the action bias (Patt & Zeckhauser, 2000). For example, a person may opt for a medical treatment rather than a no-treatment alternative, even though clinical trials have not supported the treatment's effectiveness.

The Bias in Action

Action bias is particularly likely to occur if we do something for others or others expect us to act (see social norms), as illustrated by the tendency for soccer goal keepers to jump to left or right on penalty kicks, even though statistically they would be better off if they just stayed in the middle of the goal (Bar-Eli et al., 2007).

Action bias may also be more likely among overconfident individuals or if a person has experienced prior negative outcomes (Zeelenberg et al., 2002), where subsequent inaction would be a failure to do something to improve the situation.

References

Bar-Eli, M., Azar, O. H., Ritov, I., Keidar-Levin, Y., & Schein, G. (2007). Action bias among elite soccer goalkeepers: The case of penalty kicks. Journal of Economic Psychology, 28(5), 606-621.

Patt, A., & Zeckhauser, R. (2000). Action bias and environmental decisions. Journal of Risk and Uncertainty, 21, 45-72.

Zeelenberg, M., Van den Bos, K., Van Dijk, E., & Pieters, R. (2002). The inaction effect in the psychology of regret. Journal of Personality and Social Psychology, 82(3), 314-327.

ACTIVE CHOICE

The Bias in Brief

Highlighting the fact that a decision needs to be made increases the attention paid to the decision-making process. This is especially useful for choices which are typically passive (e.g. getting vaccinated, renewing a gym plan, donating organs). Enhanced active choice refers to the presentation of options that highlight the cost of making a "no" choice.

The Bias in Action

Rather than waiting for individuals to get preventive vaccination, they could be actively asked whether they intend to get vaccinated (active choice).

Alternately, they could be presented with two options – (a) Yes, I will get vaccinated and protect me and my family, or (b) No, I am willing to expose me and my family to the risk of the disease.

The rate of getting vaccinated increased with active choice, and further increased with the alternative of giving options (enhanced active choice).

References

Keller, P. A., Harlam, B., Loewenstein, G., & Volpp, K. G. (2011). Enhanced active choice: A new method to motivate behavior change. Journal of Consumer Psychology, 21(4), 376–383.

ACTOR–OBSERVER BIAS

The Bias in Brief

A tendency to attribute one's own actions to external causes while attributing other people's behaviors to internal causes. It is a type of attributional bias that plays a role in how we perceive and interact with other people. Essentially, people tend to make different attributions depending upon whether they are the actor or the observer in a situation.

The Bias in Action

When a doctor tells someone that their cholesterol levels are elevated, the patient might blame factors that are outside of their control such as genetic or environmental influences.

But when someone else's cholesterol levels are too high, people attribute it to things such as poor diet and lack of exercise.

In other words, when it's happening to us, it's outside of our control, but when it's happening to someone else, it's all their fault.

References

Hennessy, Dwight & Jakubowski, Robert & Benedetti, Alison. (2005). The Influence of Actor Observer Bias on Attributions of Other Drivers.

AFFECT HEURISTIC

The Bias in Brief

The affect heuristic is a type of mental shortcut in which people make decisions that are heavily influenced by their current emotions. Essentially, your affect (or emotional response) plays a critical role in the choices and decisions you make.

It might not come as much of a surprise to learn that your emotions influence all types of decisions, both big and small. After all, you might already know that you are more likely to take risks or try new things when you are happy, but less likely to go out on a limb when you're feeling blue.

The Bias in Action

Researchers have found that when you are in a positive emotional state, you are more likely to perceive an activity as having high benefits and low risks.

If your emotional state is negative, on the other hand, you are more inclined to see the activity as being low in benefits and high in risk.

Affect-based evaluations are quick, automatic, and rooted in experiential thought that is activated prior to reflective judgments.

Affect-based judgments are more pronounced when people do not have the resources or time to reflect. For example, instead of considering risks and benefits independently, individuals with a negative attitude towards nuclear power may consider its benefits as low and risks as high under conditions of time pressure. This leads to a more negative risk-benefit correlation than would be evident without time pressure.

References

Finucane, M. L., Alhakami, A., Slovic, P., & Johnson, S. M. (2000). The affect heuristic in judgments of risks and benefits. Journal of Behavioral Decision Making, 13, 1-17.

ALTRUISM

The Bias in Brief

According to neoclassical economics, rational beings do whatever they need to in order to maximize their own wealth. However, when people make sacrifices to benefit others without expecting a personal reward, they are thought to behave altruistically (Rushton, 1984).

The Bias in Action

Common applications of this pro-social behavior include volunteering, philanthropy, and helping others in emergencies (Piliavin & Charng, 1990). Altruism is evident in a number of research findings, such as dictator games. In this game, one participant proposes how to split a reward between himself and another random participant. While some proposers (dictators) keep the entire reward for themselves, many will also voluntarily share some portion of the reward (Fehr & Schmidt, 1999).

References

Fehr, E., & Schmidt, K. M. (1999). A theory of fairness, competition, and cooperation. The Quarterly Journal of Economics, 114, 817-868.

Piliavin, J. A., & Charng, H. W. (1990). Altruism: A review of recent theory and research. Annual Review of Sociology, 16(1), 27-65.

Rushton, J. P. (1984). The altruistic personality. In Development and maintenance of prosocial behavior (pp. 271-290). Boston, MA: Springer.

AMBIGUITY (UNCERTAINTY) AVERSION

The Bias in Brief

Ambiguity aversion, or uncertainty aversion, is the tendency to favor the known over the unknown, including known risks over unknown risks.

The Bias in Action

For example, when choosing between two bets, we are more likely to choose the bet for which we know the odds, even if the odds are poor, than the one for which we don't know the odds.

This aversion has gained attention through the Ellsberg Paradox (Ellsberg, 1961). Suppose there are two bags each with a mixture of 100 red and black balls. A decision-maker is asked to draw a ball from one of two bags with the chance to win $100 if red is drawn. In one bag, the decision-maker knows that exactly half of the pieces are red and half are black. The color mixture of pieces in the second bag is unknown. Due to ambiguity aversion, decision-makers would favor drawing from the bag with the known mixture than the one with the unknown mixture (Ellsberg, 1961). This occurs despite the fact that people would, on average, bet on red or black equally if they were presented with just one bag containing either the known 50-50 mixture or a bag with the unknown mixture

References

Berger, L., Bleichrodt, H., & Eeckhoudt, L. (2013). Treatment decisions under ambiguity. Journal of Health Economics, 32, 559-569.

Easley, D., & O'Hara, M. (2009). Ambiguity and nonparticipation: the role of regulation. The Review of Financial Studies, 22(5), 1817-1843.

Ellsberg, D. (1961). Risk, ambiguity, and the savage axioms. The Quarterly Journal of Economics, 75(4), 643-669.

ANCHORING (HEURISTIC)

The Bias in Brief

Anchoring is a particular form of priming effect whereby initial exposure to a number serves as a reference point and influences subsequent judgments. The process usually occurs without our awareness (Tversky & Kahneman, 1974) and has been researched in many contexts, including probability estimates, legal judgments, forecasting and purchasing decisions (Furnham & Boo, 2011).

The Bias in Action

Participants in one experiment were asked to write down the last three digits of their phone number multiplied by one thousand (e.g. 678 = 678,000). Results showed that people's subsequent estimate of house prices were significantly influenced by the arbitrary anchor, even though they were given a 10 minute presentation on facts and figures from the housing market at the beginning of the study.

In practice, anchoring effects are often less arbitrary, as evident the price of the first house shown to us by a real estate agent may serve as an anchor and influence perceptions of houses subsequently presented to us (as relatively cheap or expensive). Anchoring effects have also been shown in the consumer packaged goods category, whereby not only explicit slogans to buy more (e.g. "Buy 18 Snickers bars for your freezer"), but also purchase quantity limits (e.g. "limit of 12 per person") or 'expansion anchors' (e.g. "101 uses!") can increase purchase quantities (Wansink et al., 1998).

References

Furnham, A., & Boo, H. C. (2011). A literature review of the anchoring effect. The Journal of Socio-Economics, 40(1), 35-42.

Scott, P. J., & Lizieri, C. 92012). Consumer house price judgments: New evidence of anchoring and arbitrary coherence. Journal of Property Research, 29, 49-68.

Tversky, A., & Kahneman, D. (1974). Judgment under uncertainty: Heuristics and biases. Science (New Series), 185, 1124-1131.

Wansink, B., Kent, R. J., & Hoch, S. J. (1998). An anchoring and adjustment model of purchase quantity decisions. Journal of Marketing Research, 35(1), 71–81.

ANCHORING BIAS

The Bias in Brief

Numerical judgments tend to be influenced by prominent numbers that are available in the context. These prominent numbers – called anchors – need not even be relevant to the judgment.

The Bias in Action

Two groups of people were asked to estimate the population of Perth, Australia. Before estimating, one group was asked whether they thought the population was greater or less than 50,000. The second group was asked whether they thought the population was greater or less than 10,000,000. The actual estimates provided by the second group were significantly higher.

References

Tversky, A., & Kahneman, D. (1974). Judgment under uncertainty: Heuristics and biases. Science, 185(4157), 1124–1131.

AVAILABILITY BIAS

The Bias in Brief

The availability bias is a mental shortcut that relies on immediate examples that come to mind when evaluating a specific situation.

The Bias in Action

One of the best-known studies of availability suggests that awareness of your own biases can contribute to peace in marriages, and probably in other joint projects. In a famous study, spouses were asked, "How large was your personal contribution to keeping the place tidy, in percentages?" They also answered similar questions about "taking out the garbage," "initiating social engagements," etc.

Would the self-estimated contributions add up to 100%, or more, or less? As expected, the self-assessed contributions added up to more than 100%. The explanation is a simple availability bias: both spouses remember their own individual efforts and contributions much more clearly than those of the other, and the difference in availability leads to a difference in judged frequency.

References

Kahneman, Daniel, 2013, Thinking Fast and Slow, Publisher: Farrar, Straus and Giroux; Reprint edition (2 April 2013), ISBN-10: 0374533555, ISBN-13: 978-0374533557

AVAILABILITY HEURISTIC

The Bias in Brief

Availability is a heuristic whereby people make judgments about the likelihood of an event based on how easily an example, instance, or case comes to mind.

The availability of information in memory also underlies the representativeness heuristic.

The Bias in Action

For example, investors may judge the quality of an investment based on information that was recently in the news, ignoring other relevant facts (Tversky & Kahneman, 1974).

In the domain of health, it has been shown that drug advertising recall affects the perceived prevalence of illnesses (An, 2008), while physicians' recent experience of a condition increases the likelihood of subsequently diagnosing the condition (Poses & Anthony, 1991).

In consumer research, availability can play a role in various estimates, such as store prices (Ofir et al., 2008) or product failure (Folkes, 1988).

References

An, S. (2008). Antidepressant direct-to-consumer advertising and social perception of the prevalence of depression: Application of the availability heuristic. Health Communication, 23(6), 499-505.

Folkes, V. S. (1988). The availability heuristic and perceived risk. Journal of Consumer research, 15(1), 13-23.

Ofir, C., Raghubir, P., Brosh, G., Monroe, K. B., & Heiman, A. (2008). Memory-based store price judgments: the role of knowledge and shopping experience. Journal of Retailing, 84(4), 414-423.

Poses, R. M., & Anthony, M. (1991). Availability, wishful thinking, and physicians' diagnostic judgments for patients with suspected bacteremia. Medical Decision Making, 11(3), 159-168.

Tversky, A., & Kahneman, D. (1974). Judgment under uncertainty: Heuristics and biases. Science (New Series), 185, 1124-1131

BOUNDED RATIONALITY

The Bias in Brief
Bounded rationality is a concept proposed by Herbert Simon that challenges the notion of human rationality as implied by the concept of *homo economicus*.

The Bias in Action
Rationality is bounded because there are limits to our thinking capacity, available information, and time (Simon, 1982). Bounded rationality a core assumption of the "natural assessments" view of heuristics and dual-system models of thinking (Gilovich et al., 2002), and it is one of the psychological foundations of behavioral economics. (See also satisficing and fast and frugal.)

References
Gilovich, T., Griffin, D., & Kahneman, D. (Eds.). (2002). Heuristics and biases: The psychology of intuitive judgment. Cambridge, UK: Cambridge

University Press. Simon, H. A. (1982). Models of bounded rationality. Cambridge, MA: MIT Press.

CERTAINTY EFFECT

The Bias in Brief

The certainty effect is the psychological effect resulting from the reduction of probability from certainty to probable (Tversky & Kahneman 1986). It is an idea introduced in prospect theory.

The Bias in Action

Normally a reduction in the probability of winning a reward (e.g., a reduction from 80% to 20% in the chance of winning a reward) creates a psychological effect such as displeasure to individuals, which leads to the perception of loss from the original probability thus favoring a risk-averse decision. However, the same reduction results in a larger psychological effect when it is done from certainty than from uncertainty.

References

Tversky, Amos; Kahneman, Daniel (1981). "The Framing of decisions and the psychology of choice"

(PDF). Science. 211 (4481): 453–458. doi:10.1126/science.7455683. PMID 7455683.

Tversky, Amos; Kahneman, Daniel (1986). "Rational Choice and the Framing of Decisions" (PDF). The Journal of Business. 59 (S4): S251. doi:10.1086/296365.

CERTAINTY / POSSIBILITY EFFECTS

The Bias in Brief
Changes in the probability of gains or losses do not affect people's subjective evaluations in linear terms.

The Bias in Action
For example, a move from a 50% to a 60% chance of winning a prize has a smaller emotional impact than a move from a 95% chance to a 100% chance (certainty). Conversely, the move from a 0% chance to a 5% possibility of winning a prize is more attractive than a change from 5% to 10%. People over-weight small probabilities, which also explains the attractiveness of gambling.

References
Ring, P., Probst, C. C., Neyse, L., Wolff, S., Kaernbach, C., van Eimeren, T., Camerer, C. F., & Schmidt, U. (2018). It's all about gains: Risk

preferences in problem gambling. Journal of Experimental Psychology: General, 147(8), 1241-1255.

Tversky, A., & Kahneman, D. (1981). The Framing of Decisions and the Psychology of Choice. Science, 211 (4481), 453-458.

CHANNEL FACTORS

The Bias in Brief

Features of the physical space and surroundings in a task oriented environment can either facilitate or hinder the achievement of the task. Eliminating features that hinder the task will increase the likelihood of completion.

The Bias in Action

Two groups of low-income consumers heard a (identical) seminar about the importance of opening bank accounts. At the end of the seminar, one group was given the forms needed to open bank accounts, while the second was given forms as well as a map and directions to the bank. Significantly more people from the second group opened bank accounts.

References

Mullainathan, S., & Shafir, E. (2009). Savings policy and decision-making in low-income households. In M. Barr & R. Blank (Eds.),

Insufficient funds: Savings, assets, credit, and banking among low-income households. Russell Sage Foundation Press (pp. 121–145).

CHOICE OVERLOAD

The Bias in Brief

"Choice Overload", is a term describing a cognitive process in which people have a difficult time making a decision when faced with many options. The term was first introduced by Alvin Toffler in his 1970 book, Future Shock.

The Bias in Action

In 2000, psychologists Sheena Iyengar and Mark Lepper published a remarkable study. On one day, shoppers at an upscale food market saw a display table with 24 varieties of gourmet jam. Those who sampled the spreads received a coupon for $1 off any jam. On another day, shoppers saw a similar table, except that only six varieties of the jam were on display. The large display attracted more interest than the small one. But when the time came to purchase, people who saw the large display were one-tenth as likely to buy as people who saw the small display.

References

Barry Schwartz, The Paradox of Choice: Why More Is Less (Harper Perennial, 2005),

CHOICE OVERLOAD OR OVERCHOICE

The Bias in Brief

Choice overload occurs as a result of too many choices being available to consumers.

The Bias in Action

Overchoice has been associated with unhappiness (Schwartz, 2004), decision fatigue, going with the default option, as well as choice deferral—avoiding making a decision altogether, such as not buying a product (Iyengar & Lepper, 2000).

Many different factors may contribute to perceived choice overload, including the number of options and attributes, time constraints, decision accountability, alignability and complementarity of options, consumers' preference uncertainty, among other factors (Chernev et al., 2015).

References

Chernev, A., Böckenholt, U., & Goodman, J. (2015). Choice overload: A conceptual review and meta-analysis. Journal of Consumer Psychology, 25(2), 333-358.

Hadar, L., & Sood, S. (2014). When knowledge is demotivating: Subjective knowledge and choice overload. Psychological Science, 25(9), 1739-1747.

Iyengar, S., & Lepper, M. (2000). When choice is demotivating: Can one desire too much of a good thing? Journal of Personality and Social Psychology, 79, 995-1006.

Johnson, E. J., Shu, S. B., Dellaert, B. G.C., Fox, C. R., Goldstein, D. G., Häubl, G., Larrick, R. P., Payne, J. W., Peters, E., Schkade, D., Wansink, B., & Weber, E. U. (2012), Beyond nudges: Tools of a choice architecture, Marketing Letters, 23, 487-504.

Schwartz, B. (2004). The paradox of choice: Why more is less. New York: Ecco.

CHOOSING VS. REJECTING

The Bias in Brief
The manner in which people are asked to choose between two options can change the information they use in making the decision. In particular, asking people to choose between A and B results on their focusing on reasons to choose (positive aspects), while asking them to reject A or B results on their focusing on reasons to reject (negative aspects).

The Bias in Action
A manager is looking for hiring one of two job candidates. Mr. A is average on all four relevant attributes, while Ms. B is outstanding on two and weak on the other two. When the manager chooses between the two, B tends to be preferred over A (there are more reasons to choose B). When the manager is rejecting one of the two, B tends to get rejected more often (there are more reasons to reject B).

References

Shafir, E. (1993). Choosing versus rejecting: Why some options are both better and worse than others. Memory & Cognition, 21(4), 546–556.

COGNITIVE BIAS

The Bias in Brief

A cognitive bias (e.g. Ariely, 2008) is a systematic (non-random) error in thinking, in the sense that a judgment deviates from what would be considered desirable from the perspective of accepted norms or correct in terms of formal logic.

The Bias in Action

The application of heuristics is often associated with cognitive biases.

Some biases, such as those arising from availability or representativeness, are 'cold' in the sense that they do not reflect a person's motivation and are instead the result of errors in information processing.

Other cognitive biases, especially those that have a self-serving function (e.g. overconfidence), are more motivated.

Finally, there are also biases that can be motivated or unmotivated, such as confirmation bias (Nickerson, 1998).

References

Ariely, D. (2008). Predictably Irrational. New York: Harper Collins.

Gigerenzer, G. (2018), The bias bias in behavioral economics. Review of Behavioral Economics, 5(3-4), 303-336.

Nickerson, R. S. (1998). Confirmation bias: A ubiquitous phenomenon in many guises. Review of General Psychology, 2, 175-220.

COGNITIVE DISSONANCE

The Bias in Brief

Cognitive dissonance, an important concept in social psychology (Festinger, 1957), refers to the uncomfortable tension that can exist between two simultaneous and conflicting ideas or feelings—often as a person realizes that s/he has engaged in a behavior inconsistent with the type of person s/he would like to be, or be seen publicly to be. According to the theory, people are motivated to reduce this tension by changing their attitudes, beliefs, or actions. For example, smokers may rationalize their behavior by holding 'self-exempting beliefs', such as "The medical evidence that smoking causes cancer is not convincing" or "Many people who smoke all their lives live to a ripe old age, so smoking is not all that bad for you" (Chapman et al., 1993).

The Bias in Action

Arousing dissonance can be used to achieve behavioral change; one study (Dickerson et al., 1992), for instance, made people mindful of their wasteful water consumption and then made them urge others (publicly commit) to take shorter showers. Subjects in this 'hypocrisy condition' subsequently took significantly shorter showers than those who were only reminded that they had wasted water or merely made the public commitment.

References

Chapman, S., Wong, W. L., & Smith, W. (1993). Self-exempting beliefs about smoking and health: Differences between smokers and ex-smokers. American Journal of Public Health, 83(2), 215-219.

Dickerson, C. A., Thibodeau, R., Aronson, E., & Miller, D. (1992). Using cognitive dissonance to encourage water conservation. Journal of Applied Social Psychology, 22(11), 841-854.

Festinger, L. (1957). A theory of cognitive dissonance. Stanford: Stanford University Press.

COMMITMENT

The Bias in Brief

Commitments (see also precommitment) are often used as a tool to counteract people's lack of willpower and to achieve behavior change, such as in the areas of dieting or saving.

The greater the cost of breaking a commitment, the more effective it is (Dolan et al., 2010). From the perspective of social psychology, individuals are motivated to maintain a consistent and positive self-image (Cialdini, 2008), and they are likely to keep commitments to avoid reputational damage (if done publicly) and/or cognitive dissonance (Festinger, 1957).

The Bias in Action

A field experiment in a hotel, for example, found 25% greater towel reuse among guests who made a commitment to reuse towels at check-in and wore a "Friend of the Earth" lapel pin to signal their commitment during their stay (Baca-Motes et al., 2012).

References

Baca-Motes, K., Brown, A., Gneezy, A., Keenan, E. A., & Nelson, L. D. (2012). Commitment and behavior change: Evidence from the field. Journal of Consumer Research, 39(5), 1070-1084.

Cialdini, R.B. (2008). Influence: Science and Practice, 5th ed. Boston: Pearson.

Dolan, P., Hallsworth, M., Halpern, D., King, D., & Vlaev, I. (2010). MINDSPACE: Influencing behaviour through public policy. London, UK: Cabinet Office.

Festinger, L. (1957). A theory of cognitive dissonance. Stanford: Stanford University Press.

Strecher, V. J., Seijts, G. H., Kok, G. J., Latham, G. P., Glasgow, R., DeVellis, B., Meertens, R. M., & Bulger, D. W. (1995). Goal setting as a strategy for health behavior change. Health Education Quarterly, 22, 190-200.

COMPROMISE EFFECT

The Bias in Brief

When people choose between three options that vary along two dimensions, the option in the middle (which is average on both dimensions) tends to get chosen more often. Conversely, the likelihood of choice of an option can be increased by making it the "compromise" option. This effect is particularly strong for options where it is difficult to evaluate quality.

The Bias in Action

A gas station sold two types of petrol - 89 and 91 octane grade petrol. The sales of 91 went up after they now introduced a 94 octane grade, because 91 now became the "compromise" option.

In most coffee/soft-drink/pop-corn shops where the refreshment is offered in three sizes, the medium is the most popular size.

References

Simonson, I. (1989). Choice Based on Reasons: The Case of Attraction and Compromise Effects. Journal of Consumer Research, 16(2), 158–174.

CONFIRMATION BIAS

The Bias in Brief

The tendency to interpret new evidence as confirmation of one's existing beliefs or theories.

The Bias in Action

When asked, "Is Sam friendly?" different instances of Sam's behavior will come to mind than would if you had been asked "Is Sam unfriendly?" Contrary to the rules of philosophers of science, who advise testing hypotheses by trying to refute them, people (and scientists, quite often) seek data that are likely to be compatible with the beliefs they currently hold. The confirmatory bias favors uncritical acceptance of suggestions and exaggeration of the likelihood of extreme and improbable events.

References

Kahneman, Daniel, 2013, Thinking Fast and Slow, Publisher: Farrar, Straus and Giroux; Reprint edition (2 April 2013), ISBN-10: 0374533555, ISBN-13: 978-0374533557

CONFIRMATION BIAS

The Bias in Brief

Confirmation bias (Wason, 1960) occurs when people seek out or evaluate information in a way that fits with their existing thinking and preconceptions.

The Bias in Action

The domain of science, where theories should advance based on both falsifying and supporting evidence, has not been immune to bias, which is often associated with people processing hypotheses in ways that end up confirming them (Oswald & Grosjean, 2004).

A consumer who likes a particular brand and researches a new purchase may be motivated to seek out customer reviews on the internet that favor that brand.

References

Nickerson, R. S. (1998). Confirmation bias: A ubiquitous phenomenon in many guises. Review of General Psychology, 2, 175-220.

Oswald, M. E., & Grosjean, S. (2004). Confirmation bias. In R. F. Pohl (Ed.), Cognitive illusions: A handbook on fallacies and biases in thinking, judgement and memory (pp. 79–96). New York: Psychology Press.

Wason, P. C. (1960). On the failure to eliminate hypotheses in a conceptual task. Quarterly Journal of Experimental Psychology, 12(3), 129-140.

CONJUNCTION FALLACY

The Bias in Brief

The tendency to assume that specific conditions are more probable than general ones.

'Conjunction fallacy' is when we mistakenly believe that two events occurring together is more probable than only one of those events occurring.

The Bias in Action

The more intelligent a person is, the more rational she is. That sounds like good common sense. But unfortunately, "smarter" is not always equivalent to "more reasonable". Research suggests that intelligence and rationality are weakly correlated. Or, to put it simply, being more intelligent doesn't necessarily mean you're more rational.

As you could see, Kahneman and Amos Tversky's studies revealed that even intelligent people can have irrational thoughts and beliefs. Our own study corroborated the findings among trained banking professionals. The problem is, instead of using reason or rational thinking, we often resort to intuition when making economic decisions.

References

Gigerenzer, G. (1991). How to Make Cognitive Illusions Disappear: Beyond "Heuristics and Biases". European Review of Social Psychology, 2(1), pp.83-115.

Dudley, J. (2012). Aristotle's Concept of Chance.

Erceg, N. and Galić, Z. (2014). Overconfidence bias and conjunction fallacy in predicting outcomes of football matches. Journal of Economic Psychology, 42, pp.52-62.

Kahneman, D. (2013). Thinking, fast and slow. New York: Farrar, Straus and Giroux.

Keen, S. (2011). Debunking economics – revised and expanded edition. London: Zed, p.226.

Keynes, J. (1921). A treatise on probability. London: Macmillan.

Laplace, M. (2012). Philosophical Essay on Probabilities (1812). Dover Publications.

Luhmann, N. (1993). Risk: a sociological theory. Berlin: de Gruyter.

Nilsson, H. and Andersson, P. (2010). Making the seemingly impossible appear possible: Effects of conjunction fallacies in evaluations of bets on football games. Journal of Economic Psychology, 31(2), pp.172-180.

Thaler, Richard H., and H. Shefrin (1981), "An Economic Theory of Self-Control," Journal of Political Economy, 89, 392-406.

Tversky, A., and Kahneman, D. (1983). "Extensional Versus Intuitive reasoning: The Conjunction Fallacy in Probability Judgment," Psychol. Rev. 90, 4.

CONSERVATISM BIAS

The Bias in Brief

Conservatism describes human belief revision in which persons over-weigh the prior distribution (base rate) and under-weigh new sample evidence when compared to Bayesian belief-revision.

The Bias in Action

In finance, evidence has been found that investors under-react to corporate events, consistent with conservatism. This includes announcements of earnings, changes in dividends, and stock splits.

References

Edwards, Ward. "Conservatism in Human Information Processing (excerpted)". In Daniel Kahneman, Paul Slovic and Amos Tversky. (1982). Judgment under uncertainty: Heuristics and biases. New York: Cambridge University Press. ISBN 978-0521284141 Original work published 1968.

CONSTRUAL LEVELS

The Bias in Brief

When events are to happen in the future, people view them in terms of their higher level benefits. When the same event is to happen now, it is viewed in terms of concrete details. For events that have high levels of abstract benefits but involve a lot of concrete detail (effort), this results in a diminished attractiveness of the event as it comes closer in time.

The Bias in Action

Neel was intrigued by the possibility of learning a new language and enrolled for Japanese classes that would happen in two months. After two months passed, the inconvenience of taking public transit, purchasing books, and giving up on leisure activities seemed too much, and he decided to cancel his registration.

References

Trope, Y., & Liberman, N. (2003). Temporal construal. Psychological Review, 110(3), 403–421.

CONTROL PREMIUM

The Bias in Brief

Control premium refers to people's willingness to forego potential rewards in order to control (avoid delegation of) their payoffs.

The Bias in Action

In an experiment, participants were asked to choose whether to bet on another person or themselves answering a quiz question correctly. Although individuals' maximizing their rewards would bet on themselves in 56% of the decisions (based on their beliefs), they actually bet on themselves 65% of the time, suggesting an aggregate control premium of almost 10%. The average study participant was willing to sacrifice between 8 and 15% of expected earnings to retain control (Owens et al., 2014). (See also overconfidence.)

References

Owens, D., Grossman, Z., & Fackler, R. (2014). The control premium: A preference for payoff autonomy. American Economic Journal: Microeconomics, 6(4), 138-161.

DECISION FATIGUE

The Bias in Brief

There are psychological costs to making decisions. Since choosing can be difficult and requires effort like any other activity, long sessions of decision making can lead to poor choices.

The Bias in Action

Similar to other activities that consume resources required for executive functions, decision fatigue is reflected in self-regulation, such as a diminished ability to exercise self-control (Vohs et al., 2008). (See also choice overload and ego depletion.)

References

Vohs, K. D., Baumeister, R. F., Schmeichel, B. J., Twenge, J. M., Nelson, N. M., & Tice, D. M. (2008). Making choices impairs subsequent self-control: A limited-resource account of decision making, self-regulation, and active initiative. Journal of Personality and Social Psychology, 94, 883-898.

DECISION POINTS

The Bias in Brief

People often start consumption episodes with a decision to consume, but then passively continue consumption till they hit a constraint. Inserting an opportunity to pause and think about the consumption in an active manner (a decision point) will increase vigilance and hence, the likelihood that consumption stops. Decision points could take the form of reminders, small transaction costs, or physical partitions.

The Bias in Action

Mr. X is given a large bucket of popcorn. Mr. Y has the same quantity of popcorn in four equal bags. Assuming that they are both conscious of the need to control consumption, Mr. Y will consume less than Mr. X.

References

Soman, D., Xu, J., & Cheema, A. (2010). A theory of decision points. Rotman Magazine, Winter, 64–68.

DECISION STAGING

The Bias in Brief

When people make complex or long decisions, such as buying a car, they tend to successively explore their options. This includes what information to focus on, as well as choices between attributes and alternatives.

The Bias in Action

For example, when people narrow down their options, they often tend to screen alternatives on the basis of a subset of attributes and then compare alternatives. Choice architects may not only break down complex decisions into multiple stages to make the process easier, they can also work with an understanding of successive decision making by facilitating certain comparisons at different stages of the choice process (Johnson et al., 2012).

References

Johnson, E. J., Shu, S. B., Dellaert, B. G.C., Fox, C. R., Goldstein, D. G., Häubl, G., Larrick, R. P.,

Payne, J. W., Peters, E., Schkade, D., Wansink, B., & Weber, E. U. (2012), Beyond nudges: Tools of a choice architecture, Marketing Letters, 23, 487-504.

DECOY EFFECT

The Bias in Brief

Choices often occur relative to what is on offer rather than based on absolute preferences. The decoy effect is technically known as an 'asymmetrically dominated choice' and occurs when people's preference for one option over another changes as a result of adding a third (similar but less attractive) option.

Consider two options that vary on two attributes. A is better than B on attribute one, but not as good on attribute two. Adding a third option, B*, that is worse than B on both attributes shifts choices towards B. B* can be called a decoy because it is not really preferred but shifts choices among the other two.

The Bias in Action

For example, people are more likely to choose an elegant pen over $6 in cash if there is a third option in the form of a less elegant pen (Bateman et al., 2008).

While this effect has been extensively studied in relation to consumer products, it has also been found in employee selection (e.g. Slaughter et al., 2006), apartment choices (Simonson, 1989), or as a nudge to increase hand hygiene (Li et al., 2018). A consumer is unable to choose between two headphones. Headphone 'A' has a sound quality index of 100 and a comfort rating of 50. Headphone 'B' has a sound quality index of 50 and a comfort rating of 100. The addition of a third (inferior) headphone 'B*' with 40 sound quality index and a 90 comfort rating will increase his likelihood of choosing B.

References

Bateman, I. J., Munro, A., & Poe, G. L. (2008). Decoy effects in choice experiments and contingent valuation: Asymmetric dominance. Land Economics, 84(1), 115-127.

Li, M., Sun, Y., & Chen, H. (2018). The decoy effect as a nudge: Boosting hand hygiene with a worse option. Psychological Science. Retrieved from https://doi.org/10.1177/0956797618761374.

Simonson, I. (1989). Choice based on reasons: The case of attraction and compromise effects. Journal of Consumer Research, 16(2), 158-174.

Slaughter, J. E., Bagger, J., & Li, A. (2006). Context effects on group-based employee selection decisions. Organizational Behavior and Human Decision Processes, 100(1), 47-59.

Huber, J., Payne, J. W., & Puto, C. (1982). Adding asymmetrically dominated alternatives: Violations of regularity and the similarity hypothesis. Journal of consumer research, 9(1), 90–98.

DEFAULT (OPTION SETTING)

The Bias in Brief

Default options are pre-set courses of action that take effect if nothing is specified by the decision maker (Thaler & Sunstein, 2008), and setting defaults is an effective nudge when there is inertia or uncertainty in decision making (Samson, 2014).

The Bias in Action

Since defaults do not require any effort by the decision maker, defaults can be a simple but powerful tool when there is inaction (Samson & Ramani, 2018). When choices are difficult, defaults may also be perceived as a recommended course of action (McKenzie et al., 2006). Requiring people to opt out if they do not wish to donate their organs, for example, has been associated with higher donation rates (Johnson & Goldstein, 2003). Similarly, making contributions to retirement savings accounts has become automatic in some countries, such as the United Kingdom and the United States.

References

Johnson, E. J., & Goldstein, D. G. (2003). Do defaults save lives? Science, 302, 1338-1339.

McKenzie, C. R., Liersch, M. J., & Finkelstein, S. R. (2006). Recommendations implicit in policy defaults. Psychological Science, 17(5), 414-420.

Samson, A. (2014, February 25). A simple change that could help everyone drink less. Psychology Today. Retrieved from http://www.psychologytoday.com/blog/consumed/201402/simple-change-could-help-everyone-drink-less.

Samson, A., & Ramani, P. (2018, August 27). Finding the right nudge for your clients. Investment News. Retrieved from https://www.investmentnews.com/article/20180827/BLOG09/180829939/finding-the-right-nudge-for-your-clients.

Thaler, R. H., & Sunstein, C. (2008). Nudge: Improving decisions about health, wealth, and happiness. New Haven, CT: Yale University Press.

DEFAULT BIAS

The Bias in Brief

Automatically enrolling people in benefit programs or provident funds but giving them the option of withdrawing increases the likelihood that they will continue to participate.

The Bias in Action

Company A requires all employees who want to participate in their benefits program to sign a form and send it to the human resources department. Company B automatically enrolls all employees into an identical benefits program, but allows them to withdraw with no penalties by signing a form and sending it to the human resources department. In the long run, company B has a significantly higher participation rate in its benefits programs.

References

Madrian, B. C., & Shea, D. F. (2001). The power of suggestion: Inertia in 401 (k) participation and savings behavior. The Quarterly Journal of Economics, 116(4), 1149–1187.

DIVERSIFICATION BIAS

The Bias in Brief

People seek more variety when they choose multiple items for future consumption simultaneously than when they make choices sequentially, i.e. on an 'in the moment' basis. Diversification is non-optimal when people overestimate their need for diversity (Read & Loewenstein, 1995). In other words, sequential choices lead to greater experienced utility.

The Bias in Action

For example, before going on vacation I may upload classical, rock and pop music to my MP3 player, but on the actual trip I may mostly end up listening to my favorite rock music. When people make simultaneous choices among things that can be classified as virtues (e.g. high-brow movies or healthy deserts) or vices (e.g. low-brow movies or hedonic deserts), their diversification strategy usually involves a greater selection of virtues (Read et al., 1999). (See also projection bias).

References

Read, D., & Loewenstein, G. (1995). Diversification bias: Explaining the discrepancy in variety seeking between combined and separated choices. Journal of Experimental Psychology: Applied, 1, 34-49.

Read, D., Loewenstein, G., Kalyanaraman, S. (1999). Mixing virtue and vice: Combining the immediacy effect and the diversification heuristic. Journal of Behavioral Decision Making, 12, 257-273.

DUAL-SELF MODEL

The Bias in Brief

In economics, dual-self models deal with the inconsistency between the patient long-run self and myopic short-run self. With respect to savings behavior, Thaler and Shefrin (1981) introduced the concepts of the farsighted planner and myopic doer. At any point in time, there is a conflict between those selves with two sets of preferences. The approach helps economic theorists overcome the paradox created by self-control in standard views of utility.

The Bias in Action

The more recent dual-self model of impulse control (Fudenberg & Levine, 2006) explains findings from the areas of time discounting, risk aversion, and self-control (see also intertemporal choice). More practically-oriented research on savings behavior has attempted to make people feel more connected to their future selves, making them appreciate that they are the future recipients of current savings. In an experiment, participants who were exposed to their future (as opposed to present) self in the form of an age-progressed avatar in virtual reality environments allocated twice as much money to a retirement account (Hershfield et al., 2011).

References

Fudenberg, D., & Levine, D. K. (2006). A dual-self model of impulse control. American Economic Review, 96(5), 1449-1476.

Hershfield, H. E., Goldstein, D. G., Sharpe, W. F., Fox, J., Yeykelvis, L., Carstensen, L. L., & Bailenson, J. (2011). Increasing saving behavior through age-progressed renderings of the future self. Journal of Marketing Research, 48, 23-37.

Thaler, R. H., & Shefrin, H. M. (1981). An economic theory of self-control. Journal of Political Economy, 89(2), 392-406.

EGO DEPLETION

The Bias in Brief

Ego depletion is a concept from self-regulation (or self-control) theory in psychology. According to the theory, willpower operates like a muscle that can be exerted. Studies have found that tasks requiring self-control can weaken this muscle, leading to ego depletion and a subsequently diminished ability to exercise self-control

The Bias in Action

. In the lab, ego depletion has been induced in many different ways, such as having to suppress emotions or thoughts, or having to make a range of difficult decisions. The resulting ego depletion leads people to make less restrained decisions. Consumers, for example, may be more likely to choose candy over granola bars (Baumeister et al., 2008). Some studies now suggest that the evidence for this resource depletion model of self-control has been overestimated (e.g. Hagger & Chatzisarantis, 2016).

References

Baumeister, R. F., Sparks, E. A., Stillman, T. F., & Vohs, K. D. (2008). Free will in consumer behavior: Self-control, ego depletion, and choice. Journal of Consumer Psychology, 18(1), 4-13.

Hagger, M. S., & Chatzisarantis, N. L. D. (2016). A multilab preregistered replication of the ego-depletion effect. Perspectives on Psychological Science, 11, 546-573.

ELIMINATION-BY-ASPECTS

The Bias in Brief

Decision makers have a variety of heuristics at their disposal when they make choices. One of these effort-reducing heuristics is referred to as elimination-by-aspects. When it is applied, decision makers gradually reduce the number of alternatives in a choice set, starting with the most important one. One cue is evaluated at a time until fewer and fewer alternatives remain in the set of available options (Tversky, 1972).

The Bias in Action

For example, a traveler may first compare a selection of hotels at a target destination on the basis of classification, eliminating all hotels with fewer than three stars. The person may then reduce the choice set further by walking distance from the beach, followed by guest reviews, etc., until only one option remains.

References

Tversky, A. (1972). Elimination by aspects: A theory of choice. Psychological Review, 79, 281-299.

(HOT-COLD) EMPATHY GAP

The Bias in Brief

It is difficult for humans to predict how they will behave in the future. A hot-cold empathy gap occurs when people underestimate the influence of visceral states (e.g. being angry, in pain, or hungry) on their behavior or preferences (Loewenstein, 2005). In medical decision making, for example, a hot-to-cold empathy gap may lead to undesirable treatment choices when cancer patients are asked to choose between treatment options right after being told about their diagnosis.

The Bias in Action

In a study on the reverse, a cold-to-hot empathy gap, smokers were assigned to different experimental conditions (Sayette et al., 2008). Some smokers in a hot (craving) state were asked to make predictions about a high-craving state in a second session. Others made the same prediction while they were in a cold state. In contrast to those in the hot group, smokers in the cold group underpredicted how much they would value smoking during the second session. This empathy gap can explain poor decisions among smokers attempting to quit that place them in high-risk situations (e.g. socializing over a drink) and why people underestimate their risk of becoming addicted in the first place.

References

Loewenstein, G. (2005). Hot-cold empathy gaps and medical decision-making. Health Psychology, 24(Suppl. 4), S49-S56.

Sayette, M. A., Loewenstein, G., Griffin, K. M., & Black, J. J. (2008). Exploring the cold-to-hot empathy gap in smokers. Psychological Science, 19(9), 926-932.

ENDOWMENT EFFECT

The Bias in Brief

Endowment effect (also known as divestiture aversion and related to the mere ownership effect in social psychology) is the hypothesis that people ascribe more value to things merely because they own them.

The Bias in Action

Suppose you hold a ticket to a sold-out concert by a popular band, which you bought at the regular price of $200. You are an avid fan and would have been willing to pay up to $500 for the ticket. Now you have your ticket and you learn on the Internet that richer or more desperate fans are offering $3,000. Would you sell? If you resemble most of the audience at sold-out events you do not sell. Your lowest selling price is above $3,000 and your maximum buying price is $500. This is an example of an endowment effect

References

Kahneman, Daniel, 2013, Thinking Fast and Slow, Publisher: Farrar, Straus and Giroux; Reprint edition (2 April 2013), ISBN-10: 0374533555, ISBN-13: 978-0374533557

EXPERT INTUITION

The Bias in Brief

Valid intuitions develop when experts have learned to recognize familiar elements in a new situation and to act in a manner that is appropriate to it. Herbert Simon says "The situation has provided a cue; this cue has given the expert access to information stored in memory, and the information provides the answer. Intuition is nothing more and nothing less than recognition."

The Bias in Action

The physician who makes a complex diagnosis after a single glance at a patient. Expert intuition strikes us as magical, but it is not. Indeed, each of us performs feats of intuitive expertise many times each day. Most of us are pitch-perfect in detecting anger in the first word of a telephone call, recognize as we enter a room that we were the subject of the conversation, and quickly react to subtle signs that the driver of the car in the next lane is dangerous. Our everyday intuitive abilities are no less marvelous than the striking insights of an experienced firefighter or physician—only more common.

References

Kahneman, Daniel, 2013, Thinking Fast and Slow, Publisher: Farrar, Straus and Giroux; Reprint edition (2 April 2013), ISBN-10: 0374533555, ISBN-13: 978-0374533557

FAIRNESS

The Bias in Brief

In behavioral science, fairness refers to our social preference for equitable outcomes. This can present itself as inequity aversion, people's tendency to dislike unequal payoffs in their own or someone else's favor. The tendency has been documented through experimental games, such as the ultimatum, dictator, and trust games (Fehr & Schmidt, 1999).

The Bias in Action

A large part of fairness research in economics has focused on prices and wages. With respect to prices, for example, consumers are generally less accepting of price increases as result of a short term growth in demand than rise in costs (Kahneman et al., 1986). With respect to wages, employers often agree to pay more than the minimum the employees would accept in the hope that this fairness will be reciprocated (e.g. Jolls, 2002). On the flip side, perceived unfairness, such as excessive CEO compensation, has been behaviorally associated with reduced work morale among employees (Cornelissen et al., 2011).

References

Cornelissen, T., Himmler, O., & Koenig, T. (2011). Perceived unfairness in CEO compensation and work morale. Economics Letters, 110, 45-48.

Fehr, E., & Schmidt, K. M. (1999). A theory of fairness, competition, and cooperation. The Quarterly Journal of Economics, 114, 817-868.

Jolls, C. (2002). Fairness, minimum wage law, and employee benefits. New York University Law Review, 77, 47-70.

Kahneman, D., Knetsch, J. L., & Thaler, R. (1986). Fairness as a constraint on profit seeking: Entitlements in the market. The American Economic Review, 76(4), 728-741.

FAST AND FRUGAL

The Bias in Brief

Fast and frugal decision-making refers to the application of ecologically rational heuristics, such as the recognition heuristic, which are rooted in the psychological capacities that we have evolved as human animals (e.g. memory and perceptual systems).

The Bias in Action

They are 'fast and frugal' because they are effective under conditions of bounded rationality—when knowledge, time, and computational power are limited (Goldstein & Gigerenzer, 2002).

References

Goldstein, D. G., & Gigerenzer, G. (2002). Models of ecological rationality: the recognition heuristic. Psychological Review, 109(1), 75-90.

FINANCIAL IMPATIENCE

The Bias in Brief
Prevalence of fast-food restaurants in the social ecology are associated with greater financial impatience at the national, neighborhood, and individual level.

The Bias in Action
Study 1 shows that the proliferation of fast-food restaurants over the past 3 decades in the developed world was associated with a historic shift in financial impatience, as manifested in precipitously declining household savings rates. Study 2 finds that households saved less when living in neighborhoods with a higher concentration of fast-food restaurants relative to full-service restaurants.
With a direct measure of individuals' delay discounting preferences, Study 3 confirms that a higher concentration of fast-food restaurants within one's neighborhood is associated with greater

financial impatience. In line with a causal relationship, Study 4 reveals that recalling a recent fast-food, as opposed to full-service, dining experience at restaurants within the same neighborhood induced greater delay discounting, which was mediated behaviorally by how quickly participants completed the recall task itself. Finally, Study 5 demonstrates that pedestrians walking down the same urban street exhibited greater delay discounting in their choice of financial reward if they were surveyed in front of a fast-food restaurant, compared to a full-service restaurant.

Collectively, these data indicate a link between the prevalence of fast food and financial impatience across multiple levels of analysis, and suggest the plausibility of fast food having a reinforcing effect on financial impatience. The present investigation highlights how the pervasiveness of organizational cues in the everyday social ecology can have a far-ranging influence.

References

Fast Food and Financial Impatience: A Socio-ecological Approach Sanford E. DeVoe, Julian House, and Chen-Bo Zhong University of Toronto, Journal of Personality and Social Psychology, 2013, Vol. 105, No. 3, 476–494

FRAMING EFFECT

The Bias in Brief

Choices can be presented in a way that highlights the positive or negative aspects of the same decision, leading to changes in their relative attractiveness. This technique was part of Tversky and Kahneman's development of prospect theory, which framed gambles in terms of losses or gains (Kahneman & Tversky, 1979). Different types of framing approaches have been identified, including risky choice framing (e.g. the risk of losing 10 out of 100 lives vs the opportunity to save 90 out of 100 lives), attribute framing (e.g. beef that is 95% lean vs 5% fat), and goal framing (e.g. motivating people by offering a $5 reward vs imposing a $5 penalty) (Levin et al., 1998).

The Bias in Action

The concept of framing also has a long history in political communication, where it refers to the informational emphasis a communicator chooses to place in a particular message. In this domain, research has considered how framing affects public opinions of political candidates, policies, or broader issues (Busby et al., 2018).

References

Busby, E., Flynn, D. J., & Druckman, J. N. (2018). Studying framing effects on political preferences: Existing research and lingering questions. In P. D'Angelo (Ed.), Doing News Framing Analysis II (pp. 67-90). New York: Routledge.

Kahneman, D., & Tversky, A. (1979). Prospect theory: An analysis of decision under risk. Econometrica, 47, 263-291.

Levin, I. P., Schneider, S. L., & Gaeth, G. J. (1998). All frames are not created equal: A typology and critical analysis of framing effects. Organizational Behavior and Human Decision Processes, 76, 149-188.

FRAMING: LOSS FRAMING

The Bias in Brief

Presenting the same outcome as a loss has a greater psychological effect than presenting it as a gain.

The Bias in Action

A 3% credit card surcharge was framed as a cash discount – people who pay by credit card paid the full bill amount (which included the 3%), while people who paid in cash got a 3% discount. Now the price difference between paying by credit cards and cash was seen as more acceptable.

In one neighborhood, employees of a utility company tried to convince households to purchase energy-efficient appliances by saying "If you use these appliances, you will save $10 per month." In a second neighborhood, this statement was changed to "If you fail to use these appliances, you will lose $10 per month." The likelihood of purchasing energy-efficient appliances was significantly greater in the second neighborhood.

References

Kahneman, D., & Tversky, A. (1979). Prospect Theory: An Analysis of Decision under Risk. Econometrica, 47(2), 263–291.

FRAMING: PAY-PER-DAY

The Bias in Brief
Presenting a large dollar amount as an equivalent number of dollars per day could increase the acceptability of this expense. However, this effect reverses if the per day expense is very large.

The Bias in Action
A charity asked individuals to donate $350 towards a certain cause. Subsequently, they changed their request and framed the money as "less than a dollar a day". Donations increased significantly.

References
Gourville, J. T. (1998). Pennies-a-day: The effect of temporal reframing on transaction evaluation. Journal of Consumer Research, 24(4), 395–403.

FREE – POWER OF FREE

The Bias in Brief
The word "free" captures our attention in a powerful way. Free is in a league of its own.

The Bias in Action
Behavioral economist Dan Ariely wrote about a study in his book Predictably Irrational in which they gave people the option to choose between two offers. One was a $10 Amazon gift certificate for free; the other was a $20 gift card available for $7. More people chose the $10 gift card even though the other option provided more value.

References
Predictably Irrational, Dan Ariely, Harper Perennial; 2010

(BEHAVIORAL) GAME THEORY

The Bias in Brief

Game theory is a mathematical approach to modeling behavior by analyzing the strategic decisions made by interacting players. Game theory in standard experimental economics operates under the assumption of homo economicus – a self-interested, rational maximizer. Behavioral game theory extends standard (analytical) game theory by taking into account how players feel about the payoffs other players receive, limits in strategic thinking, the influence of context, as well as the effects of learning (Camerer, 2003). Games are usually about cooperation or fairness. Well-known examples include the Prisoner's Dilemma, Ultimatum Game and Dictator Game (Thaler, 2015).

The Bias in Action

The Ultimatum Game is an early example of research that uncovered violations of standard assumptions of rationality. In the experiment, one player (the proposer/allocator) is endowed with a sum of money and asked to split it between him/herself and an anonymous player (the responder/recipient). The recipient may either accept the allocator's proposal or reject it, in which case neither of the players will receive anything. From a traditional game-theoretic perspective, the allocator should only offer a token amount and the recipient should accept it. However, results showed that most allocators offered more than just a token payment, and many went as far as offering an equal split. Some offers were declined by recipients, suggesting that they were willing to make a sacrifice when they felt that the offer was unfair (see also inequity aversion and fairness) (Guth et al., 1982).

References

Camerer, C. (2003). Behavioral game theory. Princeton, NJ: Princeton University Press.

Guth, W., Schmittberger, R., & Schwarz, B. (1982). An experimental analysis of ultimatum bargaining. Journal of Economic Behavior and Organization, 3, 367-388.

Thaler, R. (2015). Misbehaving: The making of behavioral economics. New York: W. W. Norton & Company.

GOAL VISIBILITY

The Bias in Brief

When people are in the middle of a goal-oriented task, they work harder towards accomplishing the goal when it is in sight. Consequently, reminding people of their goal or making the goal more salient or visual increases motivation.

The Bias in Action

Competitive swimmers swim faster on laps in which they face the end point of the race, and slower when they are swimming away from the endpoint. Putting photographs of children on savings envelopes increased the saving rate of parents who were saving for their children's education.

References

Cheema, A., & Bagchi, R. (2011). The Effect of Goal Visualization on Goal Pursuit: Implications for Individuals and Managers. Journal of Marketing, 75(2), 109–123.

GROUPING

The Bias in Brief

Grouping multiple objects into separate categories increases the nature of the choice process between those alternatives.

The Bias in Action

A mutual fund company sorted their offering of mutual funds along the country of origin. As a result, their customers diversified by trying to purchase funds from different countries. When the same set of mutual funds was grouped by the industry type, diversification by country decreased, while diversification by industry increased.

References

Fox, C. R., Ratner, R. K., & Lieb, D. S. (2005). How subjective grouping of options influences choice and allocation: diversification bias and the phenomenon of partition dependence. Journal of Experimental Psychology: General, 134(4), 538–551.

HABIT

The Bias in Brief

Habit is an automatic and rigid pattern of behavior in specific situations, which is usually acquired through repetition and develops through associative learning (see also System 1 in dual-system theory), when actions become paired repeatedly with a context or an event (Dolan et al., 2010).

The Bias in Action

'Habit loops' involve a cue that triggers an action, the actual behavior, and a reward. For example, habitual drinkers may come home after work (the cue), drink a beer (the behavior), and feel relaxed (the reward) (Duhigg, 2012). Behaviors may initially serve to attain a particular goal, but once the action is automatic and habitual, the goal loses its importance. For example, popcorn may habitually be eaten in the cinema despite the fact that it is stale (Wood & Neal, 2009). Habits can also be associated with status quo bias.

References

Dolan, P., Hallsworth, M., Halpern, D., King, D., & Vlaev, I. (2010). MINDSPACE: Influencing behaviour through public policy. London, UK: Cabinet Office.

Duhigg, C. (2012). The power of habit: Why we do what we do in life and business. New York: Random House.

Wood, W., & Neal, D. T. (2009). The habitual consumer. Journal of Consumer Psychology, 19, 579-592.

HALO EFFECT

The Bias in Brief

The halo effect is a cognitive bias in which an observer's overall impression of a person, company, brand, or product influences the observer's feelings and thoughts about that entity's character or properties. The halo effect is a specific type of confirmation bias, wherein positive feelings in one area cause ambiguous or neutral traits to be viewed positively. Edward Thorndike originally coined the term referring only to people; however, its use has been greatly expanded especially in the area of brand marketing.

The Bias in Action

A study by Landy & Sigall (1974) demonstrated the halo effect on judgments of intelligence and competence on academic tasks. Sixty male undergraduate students rated the quality of essays which included both well and poorly written samples. One third were presented with a photo of an attractive female as author, another third with that of an unattractive female as author, and the last third were shown neither.

Participants gave significantly better writing evaluations for the more attractive author. On a scale of 1 to 9, the well-written essay by the attractive author received an average of 6.7 while the unattractive author received a 5.9 (with a 6.6 as a control). The gap was larger on the poor essay: the attractive author received an average of 5.2, the control a 4.7, and the unattractive a 2.7, suggesting readers are generally more willing to give physically attractive people the benefit of the doubt when performance is below standard than others.

As another example, a friendly person may be considered to have a nice physical appearance, whereas a cold person may be evaluated as less appealing (Nisbett & Wilson, 1977). Halo effects have also been applied in other domains of psychology. For example, a study on the 'health halo' found that consumers tend to choose drinks, side dishes and desserts with higher calorific content at fast-food restaurants that claim to be healthy (e.g. Subway) compared to others (e.g. McDonald's) (Chandon & Wansink, 2007).

References

Landy, D; Sigall, H (1974), "Task Evaluation as a Function of the Performers' Physical Attractiveness", Journal of Personality and Social Psychology 29 (3): 299–304, doi:10.1037/h0036018

Chandon, P., & Wansink, B. (2007). The biasing health halos of fast-food restaurant health claims: Lower calorie estimates and higher side-dish consumption intentions. Journal of Consumer Research, 34(3), 301-314.

Nisbett, R., & Wilson, T. D. (1977). The Halo Effect: Evidence for unconscious alteration of judgments. Journal of Personality and Social Psychology, 35, 250-256.

HEDONIC ADAPTATION

The Bias in Brief

People get used to changes in life experiences, a process which is referred to as 'hedonic adaptation' or the 'hedonic treadmill'.

The Bias in Action

Just as the happiness that comes with the ownership of a new gadget or salary raise will wane over time, even the negative effect of life events such as bereavement or disability on subjective well-being tends to level off, to some extent (Frederick & Loewenstein, 1999). When this happens, people return to a relatively stable baseline of happiness. It has been suggested that the repetition of smaller positive experiences ('hedonic boosts'), such as exercise or religious practices, has a more lasting effect on our well-being than major life events (Mochon et al., 2008).

References

Frederick, S., & Loewenstein, G. (1999). Hedonic adaptation. In D. Kahneman, E. Diener, & N. Schwarz (Eds.), Well-being: The foundations of hedonic psychology (pp. 302-329). New York: Russell Sage Foundation.

Mochon, D., Norton, M. I., & Ariely, D. (2008). Getting off the hedonic treadmill, one step at a time: The impact of regular religious practice and exercise on wellbeing. Journal of Economic Psychology, 29, 632-642.

HEDONIC EDITING

The Bias in Brief

People either integrate or segregate monetary outcomes in order to maximise their psychological impact. In particular:

A single loss is preferred to multiple losses

Multiple gains are preferred to a single gain

In situations where there is a large loss and a small gain, the gain should be separated from the loss (the silver lining principle)

The Bias in Action

A tire shop that charged $200 for tire replacement offered a $10 discount. This small benefit was lost in the context of the large price tag. A second tire shop instead mailed their patrons a $10 gift certificate two weeks after getting their tires replaced. By separating this small gain, they made its psychological value much higher.

References

Thaler, R. H. (1999). Mental accounting matters. Journal of Behavioral Decision Making, 12(3), 183–206.

HERD BEHAVIOR

The Bias in Brief
The tendency for individuals to mimic the actions (rational or irrational) of a larger group.
This effect is evident when people do what others are doing instead of using their own information or making independent decisions.

The Bias in Action
The idea of herding has a long history in philosophy and crowd psychology. It is particularly relevant in the domain of finance, where it has been discussed in relation to the collective irrationality of investors, including stock market bubbles (Banerjee, 1992). In other areas of decision making, such as politics, science, and popular culture, herd behavior is sometimes referred to as 'information cascades' (Bikhchandi et al., 1992). Herding behavior can be increased by various factors, such as fear (e.g. Economou et al., 2018), uncertainty (e.g. Lin, 2018), or a shared identity of decision makers (e.g. Berger et al., 2018).

Herd behavior, as the bubbles illustrate, is usually not a very profitable investment strategy. Investors that employ a herd-mentality investment strategy constantly buy and sell their investment assets in pursuit of the newest and hottest investment trends. For example, if a herd investor hears that internet stocks are the best investments right now, he will free up his investment capital and then dump it on internet stocks. If biotech stocks are all the rage six months later, he'll probably move his money again, perhaps before he has even experienced significant appreciation in his internet investments.

References

Banerjee, A. (1992). A simple model of herd behavior. Quarterly Journal of Economics, 107, 797-817.

Berger, S., Feldhaus, C., & Ockenfels, A. (2018). A shared identity promotes herding in an information cascade game. Journal of the Economic Science Association, 4(1), 63-72.

Bikhchandi, S., Hirschleifer, D., & Welch, I. (1992). A theory of fads, fashion, custom and cultural change as informational cascades. Journal of Political Economy, 100, 992-1026.

Economou, F., Hassapis, C., & Philippas, N. (2018). Investors' fear and herding in the stock market. Applied Economics, 50(34-35), 3654-3663.

Lin, M. C. (2018). The impact of aggregate uncertainty on herding in analysts' stock recommendations. International Review of Financial Analysis, 57, 90-105.

HEURISTIC

The Bias in Brief

Heuristics are commonly defined as cognitive shortcuts or rules of thumb that simplify decisions, especially under conditions of uncertainty. They represent a process of substituting a difficult question with an easier one (Kahneman, 2003). Heuristics can also lead to cognitive biases.

The Bias in Action

There are disagreements regarding heuristics with respect to bias and rationality. In the fast and frugal view, the application of heuristics (e.g. the recognition heuristic) is an "ecologically rational" strategy that makes best use of the limited information available to individuals (Goldstein & Gigerenzer, 2002).

There are generally different classes of heuristics, depending on their scope. Some heuristics, such as affect, availability, and representativeness, have a general purpose character; others developed in social and consumer psychology are more domain-specific, examples of which include brand name, price, and scarcity heuristics (Shah & Oppenheimer, 2008).

References

Goldstein, D. G., & Gigerenzer, G. (2002). Models of ecological rationality: the recognition heuristic. Psychological Review, 109(1), 75-90.

Kahneman, D. (2003). Maps of bounded rationality: Psychology for behavioral economics. The American Economic Review, 93, 1449-1475.

Shah, A. K., & Oppenheimer, D. M. (2008). Heuristics made easy: An effort-reduction framework. Psychological Bulletin, 134(2), 207-222.

HONESTY

The Bias in Brief

Honesty is an important part of our everyday life. In both business and our private lives, relationships are made and broken based on our trust in the other party's honesty and reciprocity.

A 2016 study investigated honesty, beliefs about honesty and economic growth in 15 countries and revealed large cross-national differences. Results showed that average honesty was positively associated with GDP per capita, suggesting a relationship between honesty and economic development. However, expectations about countries' levels of honesty were not correlated with reality (the actual honesty in reporting the results of a coin flip experiment), but rather driven by cognitive biases (Hugh-Jones, 2016).

The Bias in Action

People typically value honesty, tend to have strong beliefs in their morality and want to maintain this aspect of their self-concept (Mazar et al., 2008).

Self-interest may conflict with people's honesty as an internalized social norm, but the resulting cognitive dissonance can be overcome by engaging in self-deception, creating moral "wiggle room" that enables people to act in a self-serving manner. When moral reminders are used, however, this self-deception can be reduced, as demonstrated in laboratory experiments conducted by Mazar and colleagues. It is not surprising, then, that a lack of social norms is a general driver of dishonest behavior, along with high benefits and low costs of external deception, a lack of self-awareness, as well as self-deception (Mazar & Ariely, 2006).

Honesty must also be understood in the context of group membership. Employees of a large international bank, for example, behaved honestly on average in an experiment's control condition, but when their professional identity as bankers was rendered salient, a significant proportion of them became dishonest. This suggests that the prevailing business culture in the banking industry weakens and undermines the honesty norm (Cohn et al., 2014) (see also identity economics).

References

Cohn, A., Fehr, E. & Maréchal, M. (2014). Business culture and dishonesty in the banking industry. Nature, 516, 86-89.

Hugh-Jones, D. (2016). Honesty, beliefs about honesty, and economic growth in 15 countries. Journal of Economic Behavior & Organization, 127, 99-114.

Mazar, N., Amir, O., & Ariely, D. (2008). The dishonesty of honest people: A theory of self-concept maintenance. Journal of Marketing Research, 45(6), 633-644.

Mazar, N., & Ariely, D. (2006). Dishonesty in everyday life and its policy implications. Journal of Public Policy & Marketing, 25(1), 117-126.

IDENTITY ECONOMICS

The Bias in Brief

Identity economics suggests that we make economic decisions based on monetary incentives and our identity. A person's sense of self or identity affects economic outcomes. This was outlined in Akerlof and Kranton's (2000) seminal paper which expanded the standard utility function to include pecuniary payoffs and identity economics in a simple game-theoretic model of behavior, further integrating psychology and sociology into economic thinking.

The Bias in Action

When economic (or other extrinsic) incentives are ineffective in organizations, identity may be the answer: A worker's self-image as jobholder and her ideal as to how her job should be done, can be a major incentive in itself (Akerlof & Kranton, 2005). Organizational identification was found to be directly related to employee performance and even indirectly related with customer evaluations and store performance in a study on 306 retail stores, for example (Lichtenstein et al., 2010). Also, when employees were encouraged to create their own job titles such that they better reflected the unique value they bring to the job, identification increased, and emotional exhaustion was reduced (Grant et al., 2014). In some cases, identity can also have negative implications. Bankers whose professional identity was made salient, for example, displayed more dishonest behavior (see honesty).

References

Akerlof, G., & Kranton, R. (2005). Identity and the economics of organizations. Journal of Economic Perspectives, 19(1), 9-32.

Akerlof, G., & Kranton, R. (2000). Economics and identity. The Quarterly Journal of Economics, 115(3), 715-753.

Grant, A., Berg, J. & Cable, D. (2014). Job titles as identity badges: How self-reflective titles can reduce emotional exhaustion. Academy of Management Journal, 57(4), 1201-1225.

Lichtenstein, D., Maxham, J. & Netemeyer, R. (2010). The relationships among manager-, employee-, and customer-company identification: Implications for retail store financial performance. Journal of Retailing, 86(1), 85-93.

IKEA EFFECT

The Bias in Brief

While the endowment effect suggests that mere ownership of a product increases its value to individuals, the IKEA effect is evident when invested labor leads to inflated product valuation (Norton et al., 2012). For example, experiments show that the monetary value assigned to the amateur creations of self-made goods is on a par with the value assigned to expert creations. Both experienced and novice do-it-yourself enthusiasts are susceptible to the IKEA effect. Research also demonstrates that the effect is not simply due to the amount of time spent on the creations, as dismantling a previously built product will make the effect disappear.

The Bias in Action

The IKEA effect is particularly relevant today, given the shift from mass production to increasing customization and co-production of value. The effect has a range of possible explanations, such as positive feelings (including feelings of competence) that come with the successful completion of a task, a focus on the product's positive attributes, the relationship between effort and liking (Norton et al., 2012), a link between our creations and our self-concept (Marsh et al., 2018), as well as a psychological sense of ownership (Sarstedt et al., 2017). The effort heuristic is another concept that proposes a link between perceived effort and valuation (Kruger et al., 2004).

References

Kruger, J., Wirtz, D., Van Boven, L., & Altermatt, T. W. (2004). The effort heuristic. Journal of Experimental Social Psychology, 40(1), 91-98.

Marsh, L. E., Kanngiesser, P., & Hood, B. (2018). When and how does labour lead to love? The ontogeny and mechanisms of the IKEA effect. Cognition, 170, 245-253.

Norton, M. I., Mochon, D., & Ariely, D. (2012). The IKEA effect: When labor leads to love. Journal of Consumer Psychology, 22, 453-460.

Sarstedt, M., Neubert, D., & Barth, K. (2017). The IKEA Effect. A conceptual replication. Journal of Marketing Behavior, 2(4), 307-312.

INCENTIVES

The Bias in Brief

An incentive is something that motivates an individual to perform an action. It is therefore essential to the study of any economic activity. Incentives, whether they are intrinsic or extrinsic, can be effective in encouraging behavior change, such as ceasing to smoke, doing more exercise, complying with tax laws or increasing public good contributions. Traditionally the importance of intrinsic incentives was underestimated, and the focus was put on monetary ones. Monetary incentives may backfire and reduce the performance of agents or their compliance with rules (see also over justification effect), especially when motives such as the desire to reciprocate or the desire to avoid social disapproval (see social norms) are neglected. These intrinsic motives often help to understand changes in behavior (Fehr & Falk, 2002).

The Bias in Action

In the context of prosocial behavior, extrinsic incentives may spoil the reputational value of good deeds, as people may be perceived to have performed the task for the incentives rather than for themselves (Bénabou & Tirole, 2006). Similarly, performance incentives offered by an informed principal (manager, teacher or parent) can adversely impact an agent's (worker, student or child) perception of a task or of his own abilities, serving as only weak reinforcers in the short run and negative reinforcers in the long run (Bénabou & Tirole, 2003). (For an interesting summary of when extrinsic incentives work and when they don't in nonemployment contexts, see Gneezy, Meier and Rey-Biel, 2011).

References

Bénabou, R. & Tirole, J. (2003). Intrinsic and extrinsic motivation. Review of Economic Studies, 30, 489-520.

Bénabou, R. & Tirole, J. (2006). Incentives and prosocial behavior. American Economic Review, 96(5), 1652-1678.

Fehr, E. & Falk, A. (2002). Psychological foundations of incentives. European Economic Review, 46(4-5), 687-724.

Gneezy, U., Meier, S. & Rey-Biel, P. (2011). When and why incentives (don't) work to modify behavior. Journal of Economic Perspectives, 25(4), 191-210.

INEQUITY AVERSION

The Bias in Brief

Human resistance to inequitable outcomes is known as 'inequity aversion', which occurs when people prefer fairness and resist inequalities (Fehr & Schmidt, 1999). In some instances, inequity aversion is disadvantageous, as people are willing to forego a gain in order to prevent another person from receiving a superior reward. Inequity aversion has been studied through experimental games, particularly dictator, ultimatum, and trust games.

The Bias in Action

The concept has been applied in various domains, including business and marketing, such as research on customer responses to exclusive price promotions (Barone & Tirthankar, 2010)) and "pay what you want" pricing (e.g. Regner, 2015).

References

Barone, M. J., & Tirthankar, R. (2010). Does exclusivity always pay off? Exclusive price promotions and consumer response. Journal of Marketing, 74(2), 121-132.

Fehr, E., & Schmidt, K. M. (1999). A theory of fairness, competition, and cooperation. The Quarterly Journal of Economics, 114, 817-868.

Regner, T. (2015). Why consumers pay voluntarily: Evidence from online music. Journal of Behavioral and Experimental Economics, 57, 205-214.

INERTIA

The Bias in Brief

In behavioral economics, inertia is the endurance of a stable state associated with inaction and the concept of status quo bias (Madrian & Shea 2001).

The Bias in Action

Behavioral nudges can either work with people's decision inertia (e.g. by setting defaults) or against it (e.g. by giving warnings)(Jung, 2019). In social psychology, the term inertia is sometimes also used in relation to a persistence in (or commitments to) attitudes and relationships.

References

Jung. D. (2019, March 19). Nudge action: Overcoming decision inertia in financial planning tools. Behavioraleconomics.com. Retrieved from https://www.behavioraleconomics.com/nudge-action-overcoming-decision-inertia-in-financial-planning-tools/.

Madrian, B., & Shea, D. (2001). The power of suggestion: Inertia in 401(k) participation and savings behavior. Quarterly Journal of Economics, 116, 1149-1187.

INFORMATION AVOIDANCE

The Bias in Brief
Information avoidance in behavioral economics (Golman et al., 2017) refers to situations in which people choose not to obtain knowledge that is freely available. Active information avoidance includes physical avoidance, inattention, the biased interpretation of information (see also confirmation bias) and even some forms of forgetting. In behavioral finance, for example, research has shown that investors are less likely to check their portfolio online when the stock market is down than when it is up, which has been termed the ostrich effect (Karlsson et al., 2009). More serious cases of avoidance happen when people fail to return to clinics to get medical test results, for instance (Sullivan et al., 2004).

The Bias in Action
While information avoidance is sometimes strategic, it can have immediate hedonic benefits

for people if it prevents the negative (usually psychological) consequences of knowing the information. It usually carries negative utility in the long term, because it deprives people of potentially useful information for decision making and feedback for future behavior. Furthermore, information avoidance can contribute to a polarization of political opinions and media bias.

References

Golman, R., Hagmann, D., & Loewenstein, G. (2017). Information avoidance. Journal of Economic Literature, 55(1), 96-135.

Karlsson, N., Loewenstein, G., & Seppi, D. (2009). The ostrich effect: Selective attention to information. Journal of Risk and Uncertainty, 38, 95–115.

Sullivan, P. S., Lansky, A., & Drake, A. (2004). Failure to return for HIV test results among persons at high risk for HIV infection: Results from a multistate interview project. JAIDS Journal of Acquired Immune Deficiency Syndromes, 35(5), 511–518.

INSIDE VIEW

The Bias in Brief

People who have information about an individual case rarely feel the need to know the statistics of the class to which the case belongs.

The Bias in Action

A distinguished lawyer was once asked a question about a reference class: "What is the probability of the defendant winning in cases like this one?" His sharp answer that "every case is unique" was accompanied by a look that made it clear he found my question inappropriate and superficial. A proud emphasis on the uniqueness of cases is also common in medicine, in spite of recent advances in evidence-based medicine that point the other way. Medical statistics and baseline predictions come up with increasing frequency in conversations between patients and physicians.

References

Kahneman, D., & Tversky, A. (1979). Prospect Theory: An Analysis of Decision under Risk. Econometrica, 47(2), 263–291.

LAW OF SMALL NUMBERS

The Bias in Brief

The law of small numbers refers to the incorrect belief held by experts and laypeople alike that small samples ought to resemble the population from which they are drawn. Although this is true of large samples, it isn't for small ones. So the "law" of small numbers isn't really a law at all, but a fallacy. And as such, it is a law you should feel free to break.

The Bias in Action

Suppose you have an urn containing marbles—half of them red and half of them blue (statisticians love urns…especially ones with marbles in them). Suppose further that without looking, you draw 100 of them. What are the odds that about half of them will be blue? Although it is unlikely that exactly half will be blue (i.e., you probably won't draw exactly 50 blue marbles), the odds are good that it will be close with a sample of 100. With 1,000, the odds are even better—and they keep getting better until your sample reaches infinity (a fact known as the law of large numbers).

But suppose instead you draw a smaller sample, say, only two marbles. There, the odds of half of them being blue is much lower…only 50%, to be exact. And with a sample of only one, the odds drop to zero. So whereas large samples tend to resemble the population from which they are drawn, smaller samples do not.

References

Gilovich, T. (1991). How we know what isn't so: The fallibility of human reason in everyday life. New York: Free Press.

Tversky, A., & Kahneman, D. (1971). Belief in the law of small numbers. Psychological Bulletin, 76, 105-110.

LOSS AVERSION

The Bias in Brief

Loss aversion is an important concept associated with prospect theory and is encapsulated in the expression "losses loom larger than gains" (Kahneman & Tversky, 1979). It is thought that the pain of losing is psychologically about twice as powerful as the pleasure of gaining. People are more willing to take risks (or behave dishonestly; e.g. Schindler & Pfattheicher, 2016) to avoid a loss than to make a gain. Loss aversion has been used to explain the endowment effect and sunk cost fallacy, and it may also play a role in the status quo bias. The basic principle of loss aversion can explain why penalty frames are sometimes more effective than reward frames in motivating people (Gächter et al., 2009) and has been applied in behavior change strategies. The website Stickk, for example, allows people to commit to a positive behavior change (e.g. give up junk food), which may be coupled the fear of loss—a cash penalty in the case of non-compliance.

The Bias in Action

People's cultural background may influence the extent to which they are averse to losses (e.g. Wang et al., 2017).

(See also myopic loss aversion and regret aversion.)

References

Gächter, S., Orzen, H., Renner, E., & Starmer, C. (2009). Are experimental economists prone to framing effects? A natural field experiment. Journal of Economic Behavior & Organization, 70, 443-446.

Kahneman, D., & Tversky, A. (1979). Prospect theory: An analysis of decision under risk. Econometrica, 47, 263-291.

Schindler, S., & Pfattheicher, S. (2017). The frame of the game: Loss-framing increases dishonest behavior. Journal of Experimental Social Psychology, 69, 172-177.

Wang, M., Rieger, M. O., & Hens, T. (2017). The impact of culture on loss aversion. Journal of Behavioral Decision Making, 30(2), 270-281.

MENTAL ACCOUNTING

The Bias in Brief
Money that is designated toward a particular cause is more likely to be spent on that cause. Designating can be achieved by physically segregating money into separate envelopes.

The Bias in Action
Daily wage earners in India were given a savings target Rs. 40 per day. Some of them were encouraged to earmark the Rs. 40 by putting it in a separate envelope. These wage earners were more likely to save.

References
Soman, D., & Cheema, A. (2011). Earmarking and Partitioning: Increasing Saving by Low-Income Households. Journal of Marketing Research, 48(Special), S14–22.

MENTAL ACCOUNTING

The Bias in Brief

Mental accounting is a concept associated with the work of Richard Thaler (see Thaler, 2015, for a summary). According to Thaler, people think of value in relative rather than absolute terms. They derive pleasure not just from an object's value, but also the quality of the deal – its transaction utility (Thaler, 1985). In addition, humans often fail to fully consider opportunity costs (tradeoffs) and are susceptible to the sunk cost fallacy.

Why are people willing to spend more when they pay with a credit card than cash (Prelec & Simester, 2001)? Why would more individuals spend $10 on a theater ticket if they had just lost a $10 bill than if they had to replace a lost ticket worth $10 (Kahneman & Tversky, 1984)? Why are people more likely to spend a small inheritance and invest a large one (Thaler, 1985)?

According to the theory of mental accounting, people treat money differently, depending on factors such as the money's origin and intended use, rather than thinking of it in terms of the "bottom line" as in formal accounting (Thaler, 1999). An important term underlying the theory is fungibility, the fact that all money is interchangable and has no labels. In mental accounting, people treat assets as less fungible than they really are. Even seasoned investors are susceptible to this bias when they view recent gains as disposable "house money" (Thaler & Johnson, 1990) that can be used in high-risk investments. In doing so, they make decisions on each mental account separately, losing out the big picture of the portfolio. (See also partitioning and pain of paying for ideas related to mental accounting.)

The Bias in Action

Consumers' tendency to work with mental accounts is reflected in various domains of applied behavioral science, especially in the financial services industry. Examples include banks offering multiple accounts with savings goal labels, which make mental accounting more explicit, as well as third-party services that provide consumers with aggregate financial information across different financial institutions (Zhang & Sussman, 2018).

References

Kahneman, D., & Tversky, A. (1984). Choices, values, and frames. American Psychologist, 39(4), 341-350.

Prelec, D., & Simester, D. (2001). Always leave home without it: A further investigation of the credit-card effect on willingness to pay. Marketing Letters. 12(1), 5–12.

Thaler, R. H. (2015). Misbehaving: The making of behavioral economics. New York: W. W. Norton & Company.

Thaler, R. H. (1999). Mental accounting matters. Journal of Behavioral Decision Making, 12, 183-206.

Thaler, R. H. (1985). Mental accounting and consumer choice. Marketing Science, 4(3), 199-214.

Thaler, R. H., & Johnson, E. J. (1990). Gambling with the house money and trying to break even: The effects of prior outcomes on risky choice. Management Science, 36(6), 643-660.

Zhang, C. Y., & Sussman, A. B. (2018). Perspectives on mental accounting: An exploration of budgeting and investing. Financial Planning Review, 1(1-2), e1011.

MINDLESS EATING

The Bias in Brief

The expression "mindless eating" has been coined by the eating behavior expert Brian Wansink. It refers to the finding that various cues associated with food non-consciously affect the amount and quality of people's consumption. Cues often serve as benchmarks in the environment. Cues may include serving containers, packaging, people, labels and atmospheric factors. They suggest to the consumer what and how much is normal, appropriate, typical or reasonable to consume. Perceptual biases contribute to a distorted sense of consumption. For example, people underestimate calories in larger servings and tend to serve themselves more when using larger utensils, plates or bowls (Wansink et al., 2009).

The Bias in Action

Brian Wansink, the most prominent academic in behavioral food science, has faced allegations of scientific misconduct and several article retractions (Ducharme, 2018).

References

Ducharme, J. (2018, September 21). A Prominent researcher on eating habits has had more studies retracted. Time. Retrieved from http://time.com/5402927/brian-wansink-cornell-resigned/.

Wansink B., Just, D. R., & Payne, C. R. (2009). Mindless eating and healthy heuristics for the irrational. American Economic Review, 99, 165-169.

MINDSET: CHOICE VS. EVALUATION

The Bias in Brief

A mindset refers to the style with which the human brain processes information. When a person has made a large number of choices, they are more likely to view incoming (unrelated) information as a choice problem.

The Bias in Action

One group of people was asked "which of the following is more prototypical of birds?" by making choices between a large numbers of pairs of birds (e.g. "crow or penguin?"). A second group was asked to evaluate (not choose) the prototypicallity of a large number of birds on a scale.

Both groups were shown purchase opportunities where they could choose Product 'A' or Product 'B', or to not choose at all. People who had chosen amongst birds were more likely to choose, and hence make a purchase, than people who merely evaluated.

References

Xu, A. J., & Wyer, R. S. (2008). The Comparative Mind-Set From Animal Comparisons to Increased Purchase Intentions. Psychological Science, 19(9), 859–864.

MINDSET: DELIBERATIVE VS. IMPLEMENTAL

The Bias in Brief
A mindset refers to the style with which the human brain processes information. When a person has approached a large number of events with a view to getting them done (rather than merely thinking about them), they are more likely to get the next event done.

The Bias in Action
Ms. A and Ms. B both faced a job that was due in three weeks and were asked when they planned to start working on it. Prior to this, Ms. A was asked about the importance of five earlier jobs she had done, while Ms. B was asked how she accomplished five of her recent jobs.
Ms. B was more likely so start working on the new job sooner.

References

Gollwitzer, P. M. (1999). Implementation intentions: strong effects of simple plans. American Psychologist, 54(7), 493–503.

MONEY ILLUSION

The Bias in Brief

The tendency to concentrate on the nominal value (face value) of money rather than its value in terms of purchasing power.

Belief that money has a fixed value in terms of its purchasing power, so that, for example, changes in prices represent real gains and losses.

The Bias in Action

Eldar Shafir, Peter A. Diamond, and Amos Tversky (1997) have provided empirical evidence for the existence of the effect and it has been shown to affect behaviour in a variety of experimental and real-world situations.

Shafir et al. also state that money illusion influences economic behaviour in three main ways:

Price stickiness. Money illusion has been proposed as one reason why nominal prices are slow to change even where inflation has caused real prices or costs to rise.

Contracts and laws are not indexed to inflation as frequently as one would rationally expect. Social discourse, in formal media and more generally, reflects some confusion about real and nominal value.

References

Shafir, E.; Diamond, P. A.; Tversky, A. (1997), "On Money Illusion", Quarterly Journal of Economics 112 (2): 341–374,doi:10.1162/003355397555208

MULTI-STAGE DECISIONS

The Bias in Brief

Presenting the same choice as a multiple stage decision rather than a single stage decision can change the outcome of the choice task.

The Bias in Action

One group of people (A) were told they would play in a lottery which offered a 25% chance of going to the second round. At this round, they were asked to choose between:

Option 1A: Get $300 for sure; Option 2A: 80% chance of winning $450, else nothing

A second group (B) was offered a choice between two gambles:

Option 1B: 25% chance of winning $300, else nothing; Option 2B: 20% chance of winning $450, else nothing

Option 1A is identical to 1B, and 2A is identical to 2B. Yet people in group A prefer 1A over 2A (there is an illusion of certainty) while people in group B prefer 2B to 1A (now $450 appears larger than $300, while the difference between 20% and 25% doesn't seem as large). Hence, presenting a gamble as a two stage decision could create an illusion of certainty and change choice.

A group of friends are deciding which restaurant to go to for dinner. In one version, they are asked to choose between Chinese, Italian, or Thai cuisines. In a second version, they are first asked if they would like Chinese, and if not, whether they would like Thai or Italian. The likelihood of choosing Chinese is significantly greater in the second version.

References

Kahneman, D., & Tversky, A. (1979). Prospect Theory: An Analysis of Decision under Risk. Econometrica, 47(2), 263–291.

MYOPIC LOSS AVERSION

The Bias in Brief

Myopic loss aversion occurs when investors take a view of their investments that is strongly focused on the short term, leading them to react too negatively to recent losses, which may be at the expense of long-term benefits (Thaler et al., 1997). This phenomenon is influenced by narrow framing, which is the result of investors considering specific investments (e.g. an individual stock or a trade) without taking into account the bigger picture (e.g. a portfolio as a whole or a sequence of trades over time) (Kahneman & Lovallo, 1993).

The Bias in Action

A large-scale field experiment has shown that individuals who receive information about investment performance too frequently tend to underinvest in riskier assets, losing out on the potential for better long-term gains (Larson et al., 2016).

References

Kahneman, D., & Lovallo, D. (1993). Timid choices and bold forecasts: A cognitive perspective on risk taking. Management Science, 39, 17-31.

Larson, F., List, J. A., & Metcalfe, R. D. (2016). Can myopic loss aversion explain the equity premium puzzle? Evidence from a natural field experiment with professional traders. NBER Working Paper. Retrieved from https://www.nber.org/papers/w22605.

Thaler, R. H., Tversky, A., Kahneman, D., & Schwartz, A. (1997). The effect of myopia and loss aversion on risk taking: An experimental test. The Quarterly Journal of Economics, 112(2), 647-661.

NAIVE ALLOCATION

The Bias in Brief

Decision researchers have found that people prefer to spread limited resources evenly across a set of possibilities. This can be referred as naive allocation.

The Bias in Action

For example, consumers may invest equal amounts of money across different investment options. Similarly, the diversification bias shows that consumers like to spread out consumption choices across a variety of goods. Research suggests that choice architects can work with these tendencies due to decision makers' partition dependence. For example, separating healthy food menu options into different menu categories (e.g., "fruits", "vegetables") and combining unhealthy options into one single menu category (e.g., "candies and cookies"), one can steer consumers to choose a more healthy options and fewer unhealthy options (Johnson et al., 2012).

References

Johnson, E. J., Shu, S. B., Dellaert, B. G.C., Fox, C. R., Goldstein, D. G., Häubl, G., Larrick, R. P., Payne, J. W., Peters, E., Schkade, D., Wansink, B., & Weber, E. U. (2012), Beyond nudges: Tools of a choice architecture, Marketing Letters, 23, 487-504.

NARROW FRAMING

The Bias in Brief

Narrow framing, by contrast, is the phenomenon documented in experimental settings whereby, when people are offered a new gamble, they evaluate it in isolation, separately from their other risks. In other words, they act as if they get utility directly from the outcome of the gamble, even if the gamble is just one of many that determine their overall wealth risk. This contrasts with traditional specifications, in which the agent would only get utility from the outcome of the gamble indirectly, via its contribution to his total wealth.

The Bias in Action

We may be able to improve our understanding of how people evaluate stock market risk by looking at how they evaluate risk in experimental settings. More specifically, this approach argues that loss aversion and narrow framing, two of the most important ideas to emerge from the experimental literature on decision-making under risk, may also play an important role in the stock market setting.

References

The Loss Aversion / Narrow Framing Approach to the Equity Premium Puzzle, Nicholas Barberis and Ming Huang Yale University and Cornell University, October 2005

OPTIMISM BIAS

The Bias in Brief

People tend to overestimate the probability of positive events and underestimate the probability of negative events happening to them in the future (Sharot, 2011).

The Bias in Action

For example, we may underestimate our risk of getting cancer and overestimate our future success on the job market. A number of factors can explain unrealistic optimism, including perceived control and being in a good mood (Helweg-Larsen & Shepperd, 2001). (See also overconfidence.)

References

Sharot, T. (2011). The optimism bias. Current Biology, 21(23), R941-R945.

Helweg-Larsen, M., & Shepperd, J. A. (2001). Do moderators of the optimistic bias affect personal or target risk estimates? A review of the literature.

Personality and Social Psychology Review, 5(1), 74-95.

OPT-IN VS. OPT-OUT

The Bias in Brief

The default choice in any decision task refers to the outcome that would happen if the individual did not make a choice. If a situation where people choosing not to choose is high (low opt-in), making a desired outcome the default (with an opt-out) will increase the likelihood of it being chosen.

The Bias in Action

In Canada, citizens wishing to donate organs must follow a procedure to get registered. Is France, the assumption is that everybody will donate organs, but citizens wishing to not donate can follow a procedure to get de-registered. Organ donation rates are significantly higher in France than in Canada.

In country A, credit card applicants must sign a consent allowing for their mailing address to be shared on a mailing list. In country B, applicants need to sign to prevent their addresses from being on a mailing list. The average citizen in country A receives a lot less junk mail than in country B.

References

Johnson, E. J., & Goldstein, D. (2003). Do Defaults Save Lives? Science, 302 (5649), 1338–1339.

OVERCONFIDENCE (EFFECT)

The Bias in Brief

The overconfidence effect is observed when people's subjective confidence in their own ability is greater than their objective (actual) performance (Pallier et al., 2002). It is frequently measured by having experimental participants answer general knowledge test questions. They are then asked to rate how confident they are in their answers on a scale. Overconfidence is measured by calculating the score for a person's average confidence rating relative to the actual proportion of questions answered correctly. (See also optimism bias.)

The Bias in Action

A big range of issues have been attributed to overconfidence more generally, including the high rates of entrepreneurs who enter a market despite the low chances of success (Moore & Healy, 2008). Among investors, overconfidence has been associated with excessive risk-taking (e.g. Hirshleifer

& Luo, 2001), concentrated portfolios (e.g. Odean, 1998) and overtrading (e.g. Grinblatt & Keloharju, 2009).

The planning fallacy is another example of overconfidence, where people underestimate the length of time it will take them to complete a task, often ignoring past experience (Buehler et al., 1994).

References

Buehler, R., Griffin, D., & Ross, M. (1994). Exploring the "planning fallacy": Why people underestimate their task completion times. Journal of Personality and Social Psychology, 67(3), 366-381.

Grinblatt, M., & Keloharju, M. (2009). Sensation seeking, overconfidence, and trading activity. Journal of Finance, 64(2), 549-578.

Hirshleifer, D., & Luo, G. Y. (2001). On the survival of overconfident traders in a competitive securities market. Journal of Financial Markets, 4(1), 73-84.

Moore, D. A., & Healy, P. J. (2008). The trouble with overconfidence. Psychological Review, 115(2), 502-517.

Odean, T. (1998). Volume, volatility, price, and profit when all traders are above average. Journal of Finance, 53(6), 1887-1934.

Pallier, G., Wilkinson, R., Danthiir, V., Kleitman, S., Knezevic, G., Stankov, L., & Roberts, R. D. (2002). The role of individual differences in the accuracy of confidence judgments. Journal of General Psychology, 129(3), 257-299

PAIN OF PAYING

The Bias in Brief

People don't like to spend money. We experience pain of paying (Zellermayer, 1996), because we are loss averse. The pain of paying plays an important role in consumer self-regulation to keep spending in check (Prelec & Loewenstein, 1998).

The Bias in Action

This pain is thought to be reduced in credit card purchases, because plastic is less tangible than cash, the depletion of resources (money) is less visible and payment is deferred. Different types of people experience different levels of pain of paying, which can affect spending decisions. Tightwads, for instance, experience more of this pain than spendthrifts. As a result, tightwads are particularly sensitive to marketing contexts that make spending less painful (Rick, 2018). (See also mental accounting.)

References

Prelec, D., & Loewenstein, G. (1998). The red and the black: Mental accounting of savings and debt. Marketing Science, 17(1), 4-28.

Rick, S. I. (2018). Tightwads and spendthrifts: An interdisciplinary review. Financial Planning Review, 1(1-2), e1010. Retrieved from https://doi.org/10.1002/cfp2.1010.

Zellermayer, O. (1996). The pain of paying. (Doctoral dissertation). Department of Social and Decision Sciences, Carnegie Mellon University, Pittsburgh, PA.

PAYMENT DEPRECIATION

The Bias in Brief
The pain of payment decreases as time passes from the payment. As a result, the strength of the sunk cost effect (a pressure to consume events that have been prepaid for) decreases with time.

The Bias in Action
The attendance rates at a physical fitness centre gradually decline from the time of making an annual membership payment. On the other hand, patrons who make monthly payments show a more stable attendance rate as a function of time.

References
Gourville, J. T., & Soman, D. (1998). Payment depreciation: The behavioral effects of temporally separating payments from consumption. Journal of Consumer Research, 25(2), 160–174.

PERCEIVED PROGRESS

The Bias in Brief

People in a goal-oriented task are more motivated to accomplish the task when they receive feedback about the progress they have made. Their motivation is driven not only by actual levels of progress, but also by their perception of progress.

The Bias in Action

People waiting in a long queue were more likely to continue waiting when the queue took the form of a line that moved as some people were being served, rather than that of a take-a-number-and-wait queue.

Two groups of people were given 400 lines of text to proofread. The first group received 20 pages of 20 lines each; the second group received 40 pages of 10 lines each. Members of the second group found themselves working faster, had a greater perception of progress, and hence were more likely to finish the task.

References

Zhou, R., & Soman, D. (2003). Looking back: Exploring the psychology of queuing and the effect of the number of people behind. Journal of Consumer Research, 29(4), 517–530.

PLANNING FALLACY

The Bias in Brief

Overly optimistic forecasts of the outcome of projects are found everywhere. Planning fallacy refers to plans and forecasts that are unrealistically close to best-case scenarios, which could be improved by consulting the statistics of similar cases

The Bias in Action

A 2005 study examined rail projects undertaken worldwide between 1969 and 1998. In more than 90% of the cases, the number of passengers projected to use the system was overestimated. Even though these passenger shortfalls were widely publicized, forecasts did not improve over those thirty years; on average, planners overestimated how many people would use the new rail projects by 106%, and the average cost overrun was 45%. As more evidence accumulated, the experts did not become more reliant on it.

References

Kahneman, Daniel, 2013, Thinking Fast and Slow, Publisher: Farrar, Straus and Giroux; Reprint edition (2 April 2013), ISBN-10: 0374533555, ISBN-13: 978-0374533557

PRE-COMMITMENT

The Bias in Brief
Humans need a continuous and consistent self-image (Cialdini, 2008). In an effort to align future behavior, being consistent is best achieved by making a commitment. Thus, pre-committing to a goal is one of the most frequently applied behavioral devices to achieve positive change. Committing to a specific future action (e.g. staying healthy by going to the gym) at a particular time (e.g. at 7am on Mondays, Wednesdays and Fridays) tends to better motivate action while also reducing procrastination (Sunstein, 2014).

When people view events that are in the future, they are more likely to be rational and wise about their choices. When the same events are in the present, people act impulsively and make foolish choices. Therefore, the best way of nudging people to make wise choices is to ask them to commit to making those choices for the future.

The Bias in Action

Employees in an organization were asked if they would like to increase their savings rate in the future. Most agreed, and committed to setting aside a proportion of their future salary increase into a separate savings account. These people who were asked to save-more-in-future saved significantly more than people who worked with a traditional financial advisor.

The 'Save More Tomorrow' program (Thaler & Benartzi, 2004), aimed at helping employees save more money, illustrates pre-commitment alongside other ideas from behavioral economics. The program gives employees the option of pre-committing to a gradual increase in their savings rate in the future, each time they get a raise. The program also avoids the perception of loss that would be felt with a reduction in disposable income, because consumers commit to saving future increases in income. People's inertia makes it more likely that they stick with the program, because they have to opt out to leave.

References

Thaler, R. H., & Benartzi, S. (2004). Save More Tomorrow: Using Behavioral Economics to Increase Employee Saving. Journal of Political Economy, 112(1), S164–S187.

Cialdini, R.B. (2008). Influence: Science and Practice, 5th ed. Boston: Pearson.

Sunstein, C. R. (2014). Nudging: A very short guide. Journal of Consumer Policy, 37(4), 583-588.

Thaler, R. H., & Benartzi, S. (2004). Save More Tomorrow: Using behavioral economics to increase employee saving. Journal of Political Economy, 112, S164-S187.

PREFERENCE

The Bias in Brief

In economics, preferences are evident in theoretically optimal choices or real (behavioral) choices when people decide between alternatives. Preferences also imply an ordering of different options in terms of expected levels of happiness, gratification, utility, etc. (Arrow, 1958). Preferences are sometimes elicited in survey research, which may be associated with a range of problems, such as the hypothetical bias, when stated preferences are different from those expressed in actual choices.

The Bias in Action

Armin Falk and colleagues have developed cross-culturally valid survey questions that are good predictors of preferences in behavioral experiments. These include questions about risk taking (see prospect theory), social preferences (e.g. about reciprocity) and time discounting (Falk et al., 2012).

References

Arrow, K. (1958). Utilities, attitudes, choices: A review note. Econometrica, 26 (1): 1-23.

Falk, A., Becker, A., Dohmen, T., Huffman, D. & Sunde, U. (2012). An experimentally validated preference module. Retrieved from http://www.eea-esem.com/files/papers/eea-esem/ 2012/2688/FalkEtAl2012.pdf.

PREFERENCE REVERSAL

The Bias in Brief

Preference reversal (Lichtenstein & Slovic, 1973) refers to a change in the relative frequency by which one option is favored over another in behavioral experiments, as evident in the less-is-better-effect or ratio bias, for example, or framing effects more generally.

The Bias in Action

Preference reversals contradict the predictions of rational choice

References

Lichtenstein, S., & Slovic, P. (1973). Reversals of preference between bids and choices in gambling decisions. Journal of Experimental Psychology, 89(1), 46-55.

PRIMING (CONCEPTUAL)

The Bias in Brief

Conceptual priming is a technique and process applied in psychology that engages people in a task or exposes them to stimuli. The prime consists of meanings (e.g. words) that activate associated memories (schema, stereotypes, attitudes, etc.). This process may then influence people's performance on a subsequent task (Tulving et al., 1982).

The Bias in Action

For example, one study primed consumers with words representing either 'prestige' US retail brands (Tiffany, Neiman Marcus, and Nordstrom) or 'thrift' brands (Wal-Mart, Kmart, and Dollar Store). In an ostensibly unrelated task, participants primed with prestige names then gave higher preference ratings to prestige as opposed to thrift product options (Chartrand et al., 2008). Conceptual priming is different from processes that do not rely on activating meanings, such as perceptual priming (priming similar forms), the mere exposure effect (repeated exposure increases liking), affective priming (subliminal exposure to stimuli evokes positive or negative emotions) (Murphy & Zajonc, 1993), or the perception-behavior link (e.g. mimicry) (Chartrand & Bargh, 1999).

The technique of conceptual priming has become a promising approach in the field of economics, particularly in the study of the economic effects of social identity (see identity economics) and social norms (Cohn & Maréchal, 2016).

References

Chartrand, T. L., & Bargh, J. A. (1999). The chameleon effect: The perception-behavior link and social interaction. Journal of Personality and Social Psychology, 76(6), 893-910.

Chartrand, T. L., Huber, J., Shiv, B., & Tanner, R. (2008). Nonconscious goals and consumer choice. Journal of Consumer Research, 35, 189-201.

Cohn, A., & Maréchal, M. A. (2016). Priming in economics. Current Opinion in Psychology, 12, 17-21.

Murphy, S. T., & Zajonc, R. B. (1993). Affect, cognition, and awareness: Affective priming with optimal and suboptimal stimulus exposures. Journal of Personality and Social Psychology, 64, 723-729.

Tulving, E., Schacter, D. L., & Stark, H. A. (1982). Priming effects in word fragment completion are independent of recognition memory. Journal of Experimental Psychology: Learning, Memory and Cognition, 8(4), 336-342.

PRIMING EFFECT

The Bias in Brief

Our thoughts and our behavior are influenced, much more than we know or want, by the environment of the moment.

The Bias in Action

Consider these two questions: Was Gandhi more or less than 144 years old when he died? How old was Gandhi when he died? Did you produce your estimate by adjusting down from 144? Probably not, but the absurdly high number still affected your estimate. My hunch was that anchoring is a case of suggestion. This is the word we use when someone causes us to see, hear, or feel something by merely bringing it to mind. For example, the question "Do you now feel a slight numbness in your left leg?" always prompts quite a few people to report that their left leg does indeed feel a little strange.

References

Kahneman, Daniel, 2013, Thinking Fast and Slow, Publisher: Farrar, Straus and Giroux; Reprint edition (2 April 2013), ISBN-10: 0374533555, ISBN-13: 978-0374533557

(MYOPIC) PROCRASTINATION

The Bias in Brief

People often put off decisions, which may be due to self-control problems (leading to present bias), inertia, or the complexity of decision making (see choice overload).

The Bias in Action

Various nudge tools, such as pre-commitment, can be used to help individuals overcome procrastination. Choice architects can also help by providing a limited time window for action (see scarcity) or a focus on satisficing (Johnson et al., 2012).

References

Johnson, E. J., Shu, S. B., Dellaert, B. G.C., Fox, C. R., Goldstein, D. G., Häubl, G., Larrick, R. P., Payne, J. W., Peters, E., Schkade, D., Wansink, B., & Weber, E. U. (2012), Beyond nudges: Tools of a choice architecture, Marketing Letters, 23, 487-504.

PROJECTION BIAS

The Bias in Brief

In behavioral economics, projection bias refers to people's assumption that their tastes or preferences will remain the same over time (Loewenstein et al., 2003). Both transient preferences in the short-term (e.g. due to hunger or weather conditions) and long-term changes in tastes can lead to this bias.

The Bias in Action

For example, people may overestimate the positive impact of a career promotion due to an under-appreciation of (hedonic) adaptation, put above-optimal variety in their planning for future consumption (see diversification bias), or underestimate the future selling price of an item by not taking into account the endowment effect. Consumers' under-appreciation of habit formation (associated with higher consumption levels over time) may lead to projection bias in planning for the future, such as retirement savings. Projection bias also affects choices in other settings, such as medical decisions (Loewenstein, 2005), gym attendance (Acland & Levy, 2015), catalog orders (Conlin et al., 2007), as well as car and housing markets (Busse et al., 2012).

References

Acland, D., & Levy, M. R. (2015). Naiveté, projection bias, and habit formation in gym attendance. Management Science, 61(1), 146-160.

Busse, M. R., Pope, D. G., Pope, J. C., & Silva-Risson, J. (2012). Projection bias in the housing and car markets. NBER Working Paper. Retrieved from https://www.nber.org/papers/w18212.

Conlin, M., O'Donoghue, T., & Vogelsang, T. J. (2007). Projection bias in catalog orders. American Economic Review, 97(4), 1217-1249.

Loewenstein, G. (2005). Projection bias in medical decision making. Medical Decision Making, 25(1), 96-105.

Loewenstein, G., O'Donoghue, T., & Rabin, M. (2003). Projection bias in predicting future utility. Quarterly Journal of Economics, 118(4), 1209-1248.

REPRESENTATIVENESS HEURISTIC

The Bias in Brief

The representativeness heuristic is involved when someone says "She will win the election; you can see she is a winner" or "He won't go far as an academic; too many tattoos." We rely on representativeness when we judge the potential leadership of a candidate for office by the shape of his chin or the forcefulness of his speeches.

The Bias in Action

Michael Lewis's bestselling 'Moneyball' is a story about the inefficiency of this mode of prediction. Professional baseball scouts traditionally forecast the success of possible players in part by their build and look. The hero of Lewis's book is Billy Beane, the manager of the Oakland A's, who made the unpopular decision to overrule his scouts and to select players by the statistics of past performance. The players the A's picked were inexpensive, because other teams had rejected them for not looking the part. The team soon achieved excellent results at low cost.

References

Kahneman, Daniel, 2013, Thinking Fast and Slow, Publisher: Farrar, Straus and Giroux; Reprint edition (2 April 2013), ISBN-10: 0374533555, ISBN-13: 978-0374533557

SALIENCE – SELF IDENTITY

The Bias in Brief
Any intervention that increases one's identity as a virtuous person increases the likelihood that they will make virtuous choices. However, it is important that the intervention happens before the choices have to be made.

The Bias in Action
People often misreport (cheat) in domains ranging from tax forms to insurance claims. In most of these situations, people have to sign and declare that the contents of the form are true – but the declaration is made at the end of the form, after all the reporting has been done. When the declaration is made prior to the reporting, the extent of misreporting and cheating significantly declines.

References
Shu, L. L., Mazar, N., Gino, F., Ariely, D., & Bazerman, M. H. (2012). Signing at the beginning

makes ethics salient and decreases dishonest self-reports in comparison to signing at the end. Proceedings of the National Academy of Sciences, 109(38), 15197–15200.

SALIENCE - THE PAIN OF PAYMENT

The Bias in Brief
In addition to the negativity of paying a certain amount, the manner in which the payment is made can create further negativity. Certain methods of payment that are extremely salient (e.g. cash or cheque) feel more painful than others that are not as salient (e.g. auto-pay or direct debit). The pain of payment determines the willingness to spend.

The Bias in Action
When a Laundromat changed from accepting cash to accepting prepaid cards, the number of people running multiple loads of laundry increased. When a cafeteria in Hong Kong moved from accepting cash to accepting a prepaid electronic card the sales of desserts and beverages increased.

References
Soman, D. (2001). Effects of payment mechanism on spending behavior: The role of rehearsal and

immediacy of payments. Journal of Consumer Research, 27(4), 460–474.

SCARCITY (PSYCHOLOGY OF)

The Bias in Brief

People have a "mental bandwidth," or brainpower, made up of attention, cognition, and self-control (Mullainathan & Sharif, 2013), which consists of finite resources that may become reduced or depleted. The scarcity mindset entails a feeling of not having enough of something. According to Mullainathan and Sharif, anyone can experience cognitive scarcity, but it is particularly pronounced for people living in poverty. On the positive side, this may induce limited focus that can be used productively. The downside is 'tunneling', which inhibits the cognitive power needed to solve problems, reason, or retain information. Reduced bandwidth also impairs executive control, compromising people's ability to plan and increasing impulsiveness whereby the focus becomes immediate—put food on the table, find shelter, or pay the utility bill (cf present bias).

The Bias in Action

The financial and life worries associated with poverty, and the difficult tradeoffs low-income individuals must make on a regular basis, all reduce their cognitive capacity. Limits on self-control or planning may lead some individuals to sacrifice future rewards in favor of short-term needs. Procrastination over important tasks is also more likely, as is avoidance of expressing negative emotions.

References

Mullainathan, S., & Sharif, E. (2013). Scarcity: Why having too little means so much. London: Allen Lane.

SOCIAL NORMS

The Bias in Brief
Making a commitment in the presence of peers increases the likelihood that the commitment will be followed by appropriate action. Also, the presence of peers who have high levels of accomplishment increase the motivation to similarly increase accomplishment.

The Bias in Action
Members of a self-help group savings program increase their savings rate when their peers routinely met to discuss progress and outcomes. Households in the UK were sent letters encouraging them to pay taxes on time. When these letters included a statement of peer performance (e.g. "9/10 people in the UK pay their taxes on time") the letters were more effective.

References
Kast, F., Meier, S., and Pomeranz, D. (2012). Under-savers anonymous: Evidence on self-help

groups and peer pressure as a savings commitment device, Discussion Paper series, Forschungsinstitut zur Zukunft der Arbeit, No. 6311, http://nbnresolving.de/urn:nbn:de:101:1-201204239864

STATUS QUO BIAS

The Bias in Brief

The asymmetric intensity of the motives to avoid losses and to achieve gains is an ever present feature of negotiations, especially of renegotiations of an existing contract, the typical situation in labor negotiations and in international discussions of trade or arms limitations.

The existing terms define reference points, and a proposed change in any aspect of the agreement is inevitably viewed as a concession that one side makes to the other. Loss aversion creates an asymmetry that makes agreements difficult to reach.

The Bias in Action

Reforms commonly include grandfather clauses that protect current stake-holders—for example, when the existing workforce is reduced by attrition rather than by dismissals, or when cuts in salaries and benefits apply only to future workers. Loss aversion is a powerful conservative force that favors minimal changes from the status quo in the lives of both institutions and individuals. This conservatism helps keep us stable in our neighborhood, our marriage, and our job; it is the gravitational force that holds our life together near the reference point.

References

Kahneman, Daniel, 2013, Thinking Fast and Slow, Publisher: Farrar, Straus and Giroux; 2013.

SUNK COST FALLACY

The Bias in Brief

Individuals commit the sunk cost fallacy when they continue a behavior or endeavor as a result of previously invested resources (time, money or effort) (Arkes & Blumer, 1985). This fallacy, which is related to loss aversion and status quo bias, can also be viewed as bias resulting from an ongoing commitment.

People who have prepaid for a consumption opportunity are driven to consume so that they can satisfactorily close their mental account without a loss. The drive to consume will be greater when the amount prepaid is higher.

The Bias in Action

Jack and Jill both had rink side seats for a basketball game. On the day of the game, there was a heavy snowstorm and the game was being shown on TV. Jill decided to stay home, while Jack braved the treacherous conditions to attend the game. Jill had received her ticket as a gift, while Jack had paid $100 for it.

Individuals sometimes order too much food and then over-eat just to "get their money's worth". Similarly, a person may have a $20 ticket to a concert and then drive for hours through a blizzard, just because she feels that she has to attend due to having made the initial investment. If the costs outweigh the benefits, the extra costs incurred (inconvenience, time or even money) are held in a different mental account than the one associated with the ticket transaction (Thaler, 1999).

Research suggests that rats, mice and humans are all sensitive to sunk costs after they have made the decision to pursue a reward (Sweis et al., 2018).

References

Arkes, H. R., & Blumer, C. (1985), The psychology of sunk costs. Organizational Behavior and Human Decision Processes, 35, 124-140.

Sweis, B. M., Abram, S. V., Schmidt, B. J., Seeland, K. D., MacDonald, A. W., Thomas, M. J., & Redish, A. D. (2018). Sensitivity to "sunk costs" in mice, rats, and humans. Science, 361(6398), 178-181.

Thaler, R. H. (1999). Mental accounting matters. Journal of Behavioral Decision Making. 12, 183-206.

TEMPTATION BUNDLING

The Bias in Brief

Creating a mechanism where people can only consume an indulgence while they consume a virtuous product will increase the likelihood that the virtuous product is consumed.

The Bias in Action

Two groups of people were encouraged to exercise more often. One of the groups was allowed to watch their favorite TV show only in the gym room, while the other had no such constraint. People in the first group exercised more because they could bundle their temptation along with the exercise.

References

Milkman, K., Minson, J., & Volpp, K. (2013). Holding the Hunger Games Hostage at the Gym: An Evaluation of Temptation Bundling. The

Wharton School Research Paper No. 45. Available at SSRN: http://ssrn.com/abstract=2183859

UNDERESTIMATING

The Bias in Brief

Paradoxically, it is easier to construct a coherent story when you know little. Our comforting conviction that the world makes sense rests on a secure foundation: our almost unlimited ability to ignore our ignorance.

The Bias in Action

Consider the story of Google. Two creative graduate students in the computer science department at Stanford University come up with a superior way of searching information on the Internet. They seek and obtain funding to start a company and make a series of decisions that work out well. Within a few years, the company they started is one of the most valuable stocks in America, and the two former graduate students are among the richest people on the planet.

On one memorable occasion, they were lucky, which makes the story even more compelling: a year after founding Google, they were willing to sell their company for less than $1 million, but the buyer said the price was too high. Mentioning the single lucky incident actually makes it easier to underestimate the multitude of ways in which luck affected the outcome.

References

Kahneman, Daniel, 2013, Thinking Fast and Slow, Publisher: Farrar, Straus and Giroux; 2013

WYSIATI

The Bias in Brief

Jumping to conclusions on the basis of limited evidence is very important to an understanding of intuitive thinking. The cumbersome abbreviation WYSIATI stands for "what you see is all there is".

The Bias in Action

When information is scarce, which is a common occurrence, our mind operates as a machine for jumping to conclusions.

Consider the following: "Will Linda be a good leader? She is intelligent and strong…". An answer quickly came to your mind, and it was yes. You picked the best answer based on the very limited information available, but you jumped the gun. What if the next two adjectives were "corrupt" and "cruel"?

References

Kahneman, Daniel, 2013, Thinking Fast and Slow, Publisher: Farrar, Straus and Giroux; Reprint edition (2 April 2013), ISBN-10: 0374533555, ISBN-13: 978-0374533557

NOTES

Printed in Great Britain
by Amazon